OPENING HEARTS

OPENING MINDS

Advance Praise

Opening Hearts, Opening Minds: Therapeutic Group Consultation (TGC) finds two highly respected clinicians' combined clinical wisdom and vast therapeutic acumen in a brief but highly accessible manual. In contrast with most contemporary group therapy formats and supervisory group processes, TGC possesses a unique design cultivating the psychic tastebuds of the *becoming* clinician, the clinician in *becoming,* creatively challenging the developing of a powerful and evocative *"language of feeling."*

The TGC format furthermore reflects the intentional blending of cognition *and* emotion, theory *and* action, therapy *and* education focusing on the therapist as a unique subjectivity by recognizing and encouraging the expression of authenticity, honesty, receptivity, vulnerability, and self-reflection within a securely framed microcosm regardless of participants' theoretical position! The therapeutic alliance, empathy, emotional sensitivity, and corrective emotional experience scaffold the TGC's underlying attachment theory approach, liming the participants' ability to learn from experience. Various felt anecdotal material is also included, clearly illustrating a powerful emotive process serving as a welcome counter-point to psychotherapy as a sterile and overly observed reality. Although positioned as a brief manual written for young inexperienced clinicians (but hopefully of some interest with more experienced therapists as well), the novice and experienced clinician-reader will soon find themselves in the creative-creating-affective field of two evocative clinicians and the product of a unique collaboration. This is a welcome contribution to the field.

—Loray Daws, Ph.D., Reg. Psych, registered Clinical Psychologist (South Africa and British Columbia, Canada). Practice in Psychoanalysis and Daseinsanalysis and Senior Faculty Member at the International Masterson Institute in New York and the Existential Psychoanalytic Institute and Society. Currently an assistant editor for the Global Journal of Health Sciences in Canada, evaluator and international advisory board member for the International Journal of Psychotherapy, and assistant editor for EPIS (Existential Psychoanalytic Institute and Society). He is the editor of 5 books on psychoanalysis and existential analysis, the most recent to be published entitled *Introduction to the Work of Michael Eigen* (Routledge 2022).

Becoming a psychotherapist requires us to lean into emotional discomfort, confront psychic pain, and genuinely examine our relations to self, others, and world. Being open to professional development also requires a personal commitment to taking risks in training and supervision. In their consultation and supervision model conducted in a therapeutic group format, Raubolt and Brink provide just that kind of holistic environment lacking in formal training programs. This is a highly recommended venture for therapists looking for psychological depth as a person in the role of helper and healer where authenticity, vulnerability, and existential awakenings are explored.

> —Prof. Jon Mills, PsyD., PhD, ABPP, University of Essex & Adelphi University; author of *Debating Relational Psychoanalysis: Jon Mills and his Critics.*

Raubolt and Brink show us that psychotherapy is beset by emotional discomfort, psychic pain, and fear of failure. Which is why anyone who engages in this kind of experience will find themselves, at least to begin with, imitating other people and repeating themselves (which is imitating oneself). And imitation is fear of failure. But no one can know what they can do until they have tried. Knowing is experimental, and knowledge is of the new. So we must shed the limitations of tradition, break away from institutionalized allegiances, refuse to be compromised by the past. What we must strive to do is, as Emerson suggests, illuminate the untried and unknown. Our interest should be in the birthing stage of the self. We should want nothing more than to be always beginning.

Too often, a sense of impossibility is the unwillingness to see the possibilities. There is no knowing beforehand in our field. The only use of what we think we already know is to make surprises possible. What we need to offer our patients, as well as our supervisees, are answering responses, not answers. This is the only alternative to doctrine or dogma. And this is what Raubolt and Brink are encouraging the beginners they are writing for to do. In other words, what they are encouraging them to do is to find different ways of living with themselves and different descriptions of these so-called selves. As people like Marion Milner, Winnicott, or Adam Phillips tell us, the most interesting thing about psychoanalysis is its unpredictability. It's a real risk, and that also is the point of it. We need to accept this, to not fear this, otherwise all we will ever do is repeat the past.

>—Michael Larivière is a psychoanalyst working in private practice in Strasbourg, France. He is the author of five books, the latest on Masud Khan. He has taught seminars in New York, Los Angeles, Montreal, Turin, Milan, Padua, Zürich, Paris, and Strasbourg.

OPENING HEARTS

THERAPUTIC GROUP CONSULTATION

OPENING MINDS

RICHARD RAUBOLT, PHD, ABPP
KIRK L. BRINK, PHD

Write My Wrongs, LLC, P.O. Box 80781 Lansing, MI 48908
United States
www.writemywrongsediting.com
Copyright © 2021 by Richard Raubolt and Kirk L. Brink

ISBN: 978-0-578-35795-9

No one can cure another if he has not a genuine desire to help him; and no one can have the desire to help unless he loves, in the deepest sense of the word.

—Sacha Nacht

Well, Mr. Therapist, Mr. Wise Guy, let us see what you are made of. Put your money where your mouth is. Only true emotional reality will do. The thing itself. Isn't this what you talked about all these years?

—Michael Eigen

Contents

Preface i

Note to the Reader iii

Introduction v

Beginnings 15

Principle 1: From Individual to Group Consultation/Supervision
Expanding Self-Knowledge and Experience,
Alone and Together 13

Principle 2: Harnessing the Power of Group
Guiding Energy, Power, and Effect 25

Principle 3: The Group Contract
Maintaining Promises, Honoring Commitments 43

Principle 4: Two Leaders
Exercising Nurturance and Direction, Taking Turns,
Together and Alone 39

Principle 5: Practicing Ethically, Practicing Effectively
Practicing with Integrity 63

Principle 6: The Person of the Co-leader
Knowing Strengths, Accepting Limits, and Staying Sane .. 77

Consultations 85

Coda 93

Acknowledgments 69

Appendix: Therapeutic Group Consultation Questionnaire 102

References 105

Authors' Biographies 109

Preface

Surprisingly, this preface ends up being the last thing we are writing for this manual. We originally wrote the manual exclusively in our dominant professional language as we described our model, which we have been developing over the past 30 years, Therapeutic Group Consultation (TGC) for therapists. Briefly and essentially, TGC provides voluntary, experiential learning in a co-led group with and for mental health professionals.

Along the way, we were getting feedback that our approach was too academic and even antiquated-sounding. This critique seemed to capture the missing something we were beginning to feel, so we began to change the tone of the vignettes we were using while keeping the sections about the operating principles primarily in our profession's native tongue.

After completing our first draft, we began asking members who were participating in these groups to give us feedback on what we had written and, more importantly, on what they had experienced. Little was said about what we included regarding the principles involved in this model. The most enthusiastic feedback concerned what was missing or what there was too little of: our relational interaction. By extension, this included the flavor of what actually happened in the groups as described best in the vignettes. Still, we clearly believe the vignettes "work," because they are essential examples that demonstrate and apply the principles employed in this model.

We also began hearing a choir of different group voices saying, "This is the stuff that we did not learn in graduate school," and "It is also the stuff that we did not and could not find in most of the workshops or training programs we attended which, while helpful, were not enough." In graduate school, both of us, along with our fellow classmates, learned how to do therapy—kind of. Here, we are writing from our accumulated experience about how to *become* the therapist we had dreamed of being so many years ago—emotionally alive, engaged, present, creative, and effective with the patients we treat. So, we thought it would be wise to change the preface of the manual to reflect this intention. Welcome. We are pleased to have you participate in our groups if only via reading. Actually, joining or starting your own group with our model may come later. Let's, at least, keep those possibilities open as we begin.

Note to the Reader

You are holding a unique manual in your hands (or, to be more contemporary, viewing it on your screen). We wrote it to describe our model of consultation/supervision in a manner that will approximate what members come to know experientially through TGC participation. We offer only a taste here, sometimes subtly, sometimes provocatively. Our hope is to stimulate your appetite for the full-course meal.

In the meantime, we have made few attempts to separate our authorship. While some examples will clearly reflect Richard's or Kirk's experiences, we seldom specify whose stories are highlighted. The writing styles will also reveal differences that may initially give the reader pause. Then again, group members experience these differences in personality as providing rich, textured learning.

We ask for your forbearance, dear reader, until you become accustomed to these transitions.

We are confident that while you may be confused at first, if you stick with this creative challenge, we will come to grow on you. Our consultative co-leadership is dynamic, original, engaging, and, at times, seamless—yet not without humor and playfulness.

Should this not be the case, in true TGC fashion, we invite you to question your feelings out loud. Could you be resisting something new because it's new? What happens if you immerse yourself in something that's not only different but also challenges the professional training you have undergone? Does emotional exposure, so much a part of our approach, generate anxiety and, perhaps, anger in you as well? If so, we have provided a special email address, therapeuticgroupconsultation.com, where we will answer any questions directed to us.

Remember, however, this is a manual and not a book. As such, it is more experimental, active, and directive. TGC is supported by solid academic research that underpins our clinical theory and observations. Although some readers may find this to be interesting and important information, we have chosen to focus on "how it's done" and the immediacy of critical moments that guide the interventions we provide.

Still, a few words about theory in general may be helpful here. We hold our theories lightly—or at least, we think we do. They can help us know what we want to accomplish and how. Our confidence most often, though, is the result of years of observing, personally participating in, and leading TGC groups in a variety of settings with various types of people. Theory helps us conceptualize what we see, but our in-depth learning has come from members who have responded so enthusiastically to how we practice.

One last word in this regard: We, the authors, each have favorite theories that help us organize what we see. If viewed from this vantage point, we are very distinct in how we conceptualize group behavior, for example. However, we also have such hard-earned respect for each other that when these differences surface, we look to learn from, rather than refute, what is different. In all honesty, theoretical issues rarely interfere as we seek to unpack the interactions unfolding in front of us.

We offer one simple piece of advice as you begin to read: Let go of what you think you know, and to the degree you can, put yourself in group with us.

—Richard and Kirk

Introduction

Psychotherapy has changed dramatically in the last few decades. It often has a sterile, objective feel—perhaps influenced by the quest for measurable and replicable outcomes. Therapists often advocate for using techniques and methods with little regard for the uniqueness of individuals. Seemingly, the formula has become something to the effect of, "If *that* is the presenting problem, then *this* must be the treatment we prescribe to be successful." However, a particular therapist's definition of "success" may depend upon their favored treatment model.

Unfortunately, many graduate schools restrict their teaching of psychotherapeutic approaches to symptom reduction via repetitive, standardized, and behavioral interventions. Newer therapists feel handicapped in clinical situations where their approaches fall flat, clients' resistances dominate the therapy hour, or the patient's clinical presentation is severe and unyielding (Hazanov, 2019). Fast-forward a few years, and these same fledgling therapists, still dedicated to their work, seek out advanced training. Yet again, they are met with methods that promise more effective treatment: EMDR, acceptance therapy, energy-focused tapping, etc. They, too, proclaim the efficacy of these methods and insist on their touted guidelines. As these models suffer from similar limitations, the therapists—now more experienced—run the risk of becoming disenchanted, jaded, isolated, and burned out. So, what does the research supporting evidence-based psychotherapy tell us? Jonathon Shedler (2020) reviewed studies assessing the effectiveness of therapy over the past 40 years. These studies clearly reveal the limitations of evidence-based therapy, which has become the dominant psychotherapy approach in the field. His review, for example, indicates that the percentage of depressed patients who got well and stayed well for modest follow-periods of 12 to 18 months hovered around 25%. The American Psychological Association (2013) released even more shocking statistics, indicating that 50% of patients remain depressed after treatment, and of those who do improve with treatment, as high as 40% relapse. Clearly, young, professional therapists entering the field need to learn and practice other treatment models.

Clinical supervision should seek to complement and refine psychotherapeutic approaches but often only meets the minimal standards required for licensure to practice. Typically, technique-oriented supervision is time-limited, behaviorally focused, cognitively fixated, and primarily concerned with the individual. Issues such as transference/countertransference, resistance, acting out, and unconscious derivatives (among others) are rarely addressed, since they are under the purview of psychodynamic approaches seldom still taught. Yet, at a fundamental level, the therapist as an individual—their feelings, fears, excitements, questions, and doubts—is given even shorter shrift, with perhaps only a passing comment or nod of support.

The consultation model we present here, Therapeutic Group Consultation (TGC), challenges these current supervision/consultation approaches. Central to this approach is the intentional blending of cognition and emotion, theory and action, and therapy and education. TGC focuses on the therapist as a person, recognizing and encouraging expressions of authenticity, honesty, receptivity, vulnerability, flexibility, and self-reflection. TGC accomplishes these objectives exclusively in a group context which adds depth and stability to the psychotherapeutic practices of group participants. The experiential nature of TGC also helps by providing a safe forum for therapists to learn from each other and experienced co-leaders, *regardless* of the theoretical approach they adopt.

While we, the authors, conceptualize psychotherapy from different theoretical perspectives, we agree attachment theory offers a comprehensive foundation for TGC. This theory, as developed by Bowlby (1969) and applied to group therapy by Marmarosh (2013), emphasizes interpersonal dynamics, regardless of theoretical orientation, for such mechanisms of change as the therapeutic alliance, empathy, emotional regulation, and corrective emotional experiences.

Bowlby has established that we are born with an innate psychobiological system (attachment behavioral system) that motivates us to seek proximity to significant others (attachment figures) in times of need to obtain protection from threats and to alleviate stress. Significant others influence our attachment system early on, and through these experiences, we form mental representations of the self and others (internal working models). When our interactions are not reliable, available, and supportive, we do not gain a sense of security, stimulating us, in turn, to engage in secondary attachment strategies.

These strategies run along two major dimensions: avoidance and anxiety. Avoidance based on mistrust of a relationship partner's goodwill leads to our behavioral independence and emotional distance; conversely, anxiety reflects the degree to which we worry that others will not be available in our times of need. According to Mikulincer and Shaver (2003),

The main goal of these efforts is to get an attachment figure, who is viewed as insufficiently concerned and available, to pay attention and provide protection.

The basic means for attaining this goal is to maintain the attachment system in an activated state until an attachment figure is perceived to be available and responsive. (p. 235)

Unsurprisingly, the strategies of avoidance and anxiety operate very differently. Because attachment avoidance is premised on a person's belief that proximity-seeking is not an option, the individual resorts to a defensive self-reliance. In doing so, they deny their need for and suppress any pursuit of attachment. Conversely, people using anxiety strategies seek physical and psychological closeness with others. They feel heightened vigilance regarding actual and potential threats and monitor the availability of the attachment figure. Now, how does this theory relate to the development and practice of TGC?

In his book *Secure Base* (1988), Bowlby suggests the mechanisms of change include the therapeutic relationship, which is considered fundamental in establishing a bond and providing a secure base. If a therapist and patient struggle to create an attachment, it could disrupt treatment. To this point, Bowlby has written:

A patient's way of construing his relationship with his therapist is not determined solely by the patient's history. It is determined no less by the way the therapist treats him. Thus the therapist must strive always to be aware of his contribution to the relationship…I want to emphasize that…the focus of therapy must always be on the interactions of the patient and therapist in the here and now. (p. 141)

As this description has gained acceptance, we have witnessed a growing body of research on supervision, specifically regarding the relationship between therapist and supervisor. In summarizing the conclusions of these studies, Marmarosh (2015) has written:

> A supervisor has a powerful impact on the treatment and can point out when a therapist is avoiding a patient's emotion, missing a rupture or trying to smooth over conflict rather than explore it. The supervisor who is functioning as a secure base also has the ability to help regulate the supervisee's anxieties, help the supervisee empathize with the patient, and facilitate taking risks such as welcoming the patient's expression of anger or conflict in the session. (p. 15)

We quote Bowlby and Marmarosh because they articulate many of the objectives and processes considered essential in TGC. Stated another way, they identify what therapists seek and what can be accomplished in the supervisory relationship. We believe this is even more impactful in a group setting where the members, as well as the supervisor/leader(s), activate the attachment system. Recall that two types of bonds exist in groups: dyadic (supervisor to supervisee and vice versa) and group (supervisee to group and vice versa). From the perspective of the group, a social microcosm is created where relationships are in flux. Participants have the opportunity to observe and then intervene directly with a member's internal working models.

Furthermore, the group format provides a recapitulation of the original family group such that corrective emotional experiences contribute to people building a secure attachment style in which they can internalize positive attachments. It also allows for new learning strategies that contribute to affect regulation through understanding and verbalizing emotions. This adds to group cohesion, which is considered the equivalent of the therapeutic alliance in individual therapy.

Our definition of TGC focuses on consultation/supervision provided by two designated leaders in a group whose members consist of a variety of professionally trained psychotherapists meeting regularly and voluntarily. The group's purpose is to foster the growth and development of its members as individuals and clinicians. Ultimately, the professional purpose is to enhance the treatment of the patients with whom the members work.

The presence of designated leaders distinguishes this type of group from a peer group that has no designated leadership. In TGC, the consultation/supervision occurs in a group format with some elements of a peer supervision group. Two typologies combine to encompass the central aspects of TGC: *participative*, or consultation *with a group* (members are taught and encouraged to participate to develop active group skills, leadership, and group interactional skills); and *cooperative*, or consultation *by the group* (providing collegial support, developing shared professional accountability, and offering different models of theory, style, and practice).

There are a few overarching objectives in applying attachment theory to the TGC model. After presenting a brief discussion of these goals, we will offer a video demonstration of typical TGC group interactions followed by a question-and-answer panel consisting of current and former TGC participants.

The goals of TGC are to:

1. Achieve clarity of roles, expectations, and responsibilities for leaders and participants through individual group interviews, screenings, and preparation. Prospective members are invited to attend up to three meetings before committing to membership and the accompanying responsibilities. These meetings also allow all parties concerned to review the group contract.

2. Pay attention to group interactions initiated by leader(s) or member(s) that inhibit or foster more secure attachments. Group observations are presented as comments, adherence to the group contract, and emphasis on developing a "language of feelings."

3. Explore, develop, and expand a group ambiance of safety, curiosity, and commitment. Leaders of TGC groups encourage questions, appreciate uncertainty, seek nuanced answers/directions, and value honest, open expression of both loving and aggressive feelings while remaining respectful of individual differences.

4. Provide the structure for intimate and expansive interactions with the leaders due to the dual leadership format of TGC groups. Two personal attributes are considered essential for leaders in this model: emotional availability and genuine responsiveness as evidenced through self-disclosure and a willingness to engage in the face of negative reactions. They must also maintain a consistent and reliable emotional presence when loving, intimate (libidinal) transferences hold sway.

5. Recognize occasions to enhance cohesion, take risks, and create a sense of belonging and intimacy. The direct, honest expression of emotions, thoughts, wishes, and fantasies forms openings for participants to express creativity, relate authentically, develop interpersonal trust, and feel a sense of shared purpose.

6. Pay special attention when people convey negative and positive feelings and attitudes. We consider it crucial to identify and address fears of emotional abandonment and engulfment, as they are so frequently tied to early developmental conflicts centering on attachment vulnerabilities. We use Karen Horney's template (1950) to provide a framework to observe internal working models expressed in behavior. She identified three

neurotic trends: *compliant*, or moving toward others seeking affirmation, acceptance, approval, and love; *aggression*, or moving against others to control and/or dominate with hostility; and *detached*, or withdrawing, expressed via emotional coldness or indifference. As Horney identifies them, these trends color group participation while revealing levels of attachment security and, as such, are a boon to understanding members personally and professionally.

In keeping with our TGC format, we ask the following questions: (1) What have you learned so far that might be applicable in your work or private life? (2) What has not been helpful/has been confusing, vague, or unconvincing so far? (3) How will you integrate what you just learned to improve your work and/or life? In our experience, these questions are best asked and answered out loud or in writing, either to yourself or to us at **therapeuticgroupconsultation.com** *or* **therapeuticconsultation.com**. *No, we're not kidding. Try us. We have found that seeing and hearing your own words sharpens focus and enhances emotional engagement.*

Website: www.therapeuticgroupconsultation.com
Demonstration/role playing/experiential TGC session
Q&A participants from demonstration group
Q&A experienced participants from TGC groups

Beginnings

Kirk's Story (with a Little History to Boot)

This story is about my part in the history of TGC: its origins, its development, its milestones, etc. And…well, it's also a story about me—Kirk. Those of you who are impatient or busy may be tempted to skip this section. Go ahead, if you're so inclined, but this may be the most interesting and/or important part of the manual. I will admit, though, that when I normally read something called a *manual*, I'm in a hurry to get to the main event.

How did this method called TGC get started? Before 1990, I had been in "case consultation" supervision which involved a therapist describing a patient and what we called "the dynamics of the case." The format was structured around understanding the patient's problems and the supervisor giving the supervisee recommendations. I experienced this in graduate school and at the psychiatric hospital where I worked—both in groups and individually.

Richard invited me to a group supervision led by Natan HarPaz, a skilled group therapist. He conducted this supervision primarily like group therapy, except we were all therapists, and we met once per month for three hours. This experience influenced me to become much more active in my functioning as a group therapist.

In fact, it led me to change the way I practiced, and I began seeing patients in both individual and group sessions every week.

This experience also influenced the way I conducted supervision. About 30 years ago, while I was learning from Natan about group therapy and co-leading several groups, I was approached by two therapists interested in participating in group supervision with me. Both were highly respected in the professional community, and I also held them in high esteem. Looking back, I wonder why they selected me as their supervisor. I wish I had asked them, but instead, I constructed a story or tale to explain it, as I always do.

Later in this manual, when I describe the process of choosing my own co-leader, you will see how I spared Richard the painful agony of wondering why he had been selected for the role. (See the description on page 69 of the exercise we use to help group members think about the kind of group leader they need. We did this exercise when Richard joined as the new co-leader.)

Phase One: Starting group supervision

The very first meetings involved the two aforementioned therapists and me. They had started leading a therapy group together and were looking for creative supervision. Not only did they require help in conducting group therapy, but also, and more importantly, they needed help working together. Occasionally, in group supervision, we discussed patients and group therapy interventions, but most often, I focused our discussions on the therapists themselves and their reactions to their fellow group members. I often seemed to be intervening as if in couples therapy rather than addressing how they co-led their group. Looking back, I can now see my responses, and lack thereof, to their particular needs shaped the character of this supervision model in the early stage of TGC development.

Phase Two: Guiding the group through its first potential ending

Eventually, after about 2 years, these two therapists decided to discontinue working together. One of them wanted to continue with me in this kind of supervision. I knew others who wanted group supervision, so I continued with four members and myself. I knew that together, we were constructing a different kind of supervision practice which I thought had to be experienced to be appreciated. I was reasonably sure it would be difficult to describe. I experienced it as something we were developing together, and I had limited awareness of the leadership I provided.

We established a "new" group by adding four therapists. I did my very best to help them. I challenged and confronted them in my most engaging ways. I discovered it was necessary to persist with them by pursuing more than their first answers to the questions I would ask. We discovered together the importance in exploring their feelings toward the patient as well as their formulating strategies to help the patient. I was intent on stimulating them each time with fresh, provocative ideas about who they were and what they did—or didn't do—with their patients. Looking back, I wonder why I didn't ask them to talk about their experiences, as doing so would have been consistent with current TGC practices.

I did not expect the group to last long. At the time, I was only slightly mindful that the members and I were experiencing something valuable through these group sessions, something we were not getting elsewhere or had experienced before. This "something" was elusive and difficult to describe, but the effect was life-altering. I told myself the therapists attended group supervision solely to fulfill their licensing requirements, but that was true only for one of the members.

I also told myself they were attending because it was convenient and that somebody had told them during their career they *should* get supervision to improve their practice as therapists. I didn't realize they were in the group for a variety of reasons, and again, I failed to ask them. This is a mistake I no longer make. In retrospect, I assume I must have feared their responses. I must have thought asking why they were attending would stimulate the therapists to identify what they weren't getting. I feared my questions might trigger them to leave the group or otherwise fulfill some unidentified anxiety of mine.

The group was adding members and had grown from four to six.

Phase Three: Launching the method with a group that had no previous relationship with me

In 1995, while I was supervising those mentioned in the previous paragraph, a group therapy co-leader and I were asked to supervise a group of doctoral-level psychology interns at a local psychiatric hospital.

Supervising this group of interns, yet unknown to me, was an important development in the TGC method. We took the method on the road and tested it with a group of fresh, young therapists (see Lavonne's memory of these group experiences). This provided a situation wherein the approach could be evaluated on its own merits and not based on the relationship the members had with me prior to being in a supervision group. I approached the interns with the same stimulating, provocative, and challenging methods I had honed in my established supervision group. It was evident to me in this setting that discomfort and anxiety led these therapists to talk about themselves with greater vulnerability than they had in their lives or with or about their patients. Their responses confirmed that I was headed in the right direction in creating the kind of supervision experience that would stimulate positive growth and development for therapists.

Phase Four: Starting a second group

The next major change came when a colleague, with whom I was in a leaderless peer supervision group, wanted to conduct co-therapy with me, co-lead this supervision group, and start another co-therapy group. Eventually, one of the two groups began meeting weekly, whereas they had previously met every other week. On the surface, it appeared that more often than not, therapists were joining specifically to get help with discontinuing their reliance on being in-network with insurance companies to get referrals or patients who were unlikely to see a therapist not covered by their health insurance. Some also hoped to generate referrals from other members of the group. However, once in the group, they rarely talked about either of these issues and began to enjoy the development of their relationships with other members in addition to their own personal and professional progress. My co-leader retired in 2017, and, for several months, I continued the groups by myself.

Phase Five: The supervision method matures with new leadership

In 2018, Richard and I began co-leading group supervision sessions. This invaluable partnership truly refined the TGC model of supervision. We met in 1976 and have worked in various capacities, including co-leading a therapist supervision group as well as workshops and retreats. Yet, all these activities have been time limited.

Richard thought it would be valuable to write about the TGC method. He was active in developing the questionnaire we use to gain feedback about members' experiences, and he recently initiated a third supervision group. His experience and our trusting relationship have encouraged me to develop personally and exercise my leadership in the group sessions. I know I can rely on him for advice when I'm not seeing eye-to-eye with a group member. In these situations, he may explain my feedback to the member in a different way, or he might suggest a different approach, so the member has another trusted opinion to consider. This has allowed me to be less unnecessarily cautious and, among other things, to use my humor more often and more effectively.

In a particular group session, one of the members described trying to do something with a patient that sounded very difficult, even ridiculously so. I said it was like "trying to push a carrot through a board." Richard repeated the phrase, laughing. Through this simple exchange, the member had a chance to catch her breath, and the group entered into a few precious moments of play. Later, when another member was talking about the difficulty that she had maintaining her patience while working with a patient suffering from borderline personality disorder, I gently but directly challenged the therapist to describe the borderline qualities in herself. She found this challenge provocative, challenging, and even confrontational. Afterward, they both talked about these interactions with me, clearly having experienced the collaborative, playful, kind, and even loving quality of my challenge to them. These relational experiences require both vulnerability and trust among all members, including the leaders, of the group.

Phase Six: Stay tuned. You, dear reader, are making it happen

Richard's Story

The call from Kirk surprised me, but it was a welcome surprise. We have known each other for 40 years—give or take—and we have co-led groups in the past, but that took place a while ago.

After I left a peer-supervision group we'd both been members of, we drifted apart. I pursued training and certification in psychoanalysis, and Kirk studied Radix, crisis mobilization therapy, and hypnosis.

I was aware of what Kirk was engaged in professionally, as our psychotherapy community is tight-knit and communicative. Still, I didn't know whether there was enough overlap in our fields of study to allow for a joint language of leadership, or if our dialects expressed differences that were actually more substantial than semantic. Would confrontation be valued more than understanding? Would behavioral change be the measurement of success? What about the influence of resistances, enactments, and the like, which I found so compelling, but which also sounded so esoteric? Still, I was flattered and intrigued when Kirk asked me if I would consider co-leading a few groups with him. At least, that was what I thought he asked. What Kirk really asked was whether I would be interested in interviewing to lead these groups with him.

I struggled with this request to interview mightily. I'd been the first clinician to introduce group therapy in our area, and he had sought me out for supervision in the past. Since he had known me over time and had firsthand experience of how I worked, I wondered what exactly he would be evaluating. Later, Kirk mentioned that I would lead a group session, and the group would also evaluate me upon its conclusion. Additionally, I learned there would be multiple interviews because other therapists were also being considered, but I would be the most senior. *Great,* I thought. *Higher expectations and more to lose.*

So, here was my dilemma: How badly did I want to work with Kirk again? What did I have to offer him (and the group)? What did he have to offer me? Could we work together creatively, integrating the best of our differing experiences? Could we be respectful of each other's differences in pacing and level of intensity? And, frankly, for me, was I willing to be vulnerable enough to share my life with Kirk, including what I believed in and how I lived, doubts and failures included?

I knew neither of us would agree to expectations that weren't based on authentic engagement and the freedom to agree and disagree openly and honestly.

In my estimation, working together would require the capacity to tolerate and acknowledge complex and contradictory feelings toward each other, including love and hate. Clinically, these values fall under the rubric of mutual responsiveness, empathic connectedness, and dependability, and because they reveal what I expect of myself, why wouldn't I expect them of Kirk as well?

Finally, if I were going to co-lead, which demanded more from me emotionally than leading a group alone, I wanted to know whether the strength I attributed to Kirk was real or exaggerated.

Then, there was the issue of the group interview.

I knew the only way to really find answers to my conflicting feelings would be to go through the process.

I would be evaluated by two different groups. But to use this experience, I would need to humble myself and quiet the face-saving defenses I was erecting. My identity as a therapist is tied closely to who I am as a person, so it wasn't just the therapist side of me I was putting on the line for scrutiny.

These personal issues led to damn difficult feelings and subsequent conversations with Kirk. As a result, though we became clearer about how we could work together and the fact that we wanted to, this still left me with the necessity of meeting with the group(s).

This Is What We Hear: Memories of Kirk and Richard

Almost 30 years ago, I went to graduate school to become a clinical psychologist with a focus on being a psychotherapist. Disappointingly, and also ironically, I gained almost no experience in being a therapist. Instead, I got experience in topic-focused group therapy, case management, and assessment, but in my 4 years of graduate school, I saw just one individual client. I was unprepared for my internship, where I was placed in an outpatient clinic with a supervisor who had a different theoretical orientation than me. I can still feel the tension in my body from when I met with her and tried to absorb her instructions. At the same time, I was unresponsive to her advice or approach.

At that point, I didn't know there could be another way of engaging in supervision. The model was supervisor (teacher) and intern (student). She had wisdom to impart in the form of her own therapeutic technique and approach, and I was to soak it up and repeat the process with my clients.

Then, I met Kirk. There were four interns in my group at the local psychiatric hospital. We were told we'd have off-site supervision and the group would be confidential. During that first group session, Kirk engaged us with fairly simple questions: Why did we pick clinical psychology? What would that mean for our futures? After completing four grueling years of graduate school, I transitioned from sunny California to wintry Michigan. Despite wanting to be a therapist, I had no relevant experience in the field and lacked the necessary mentorship of a trusted supervisor. I was lost. I was scared. I was depressed. "I don't know," I said aloud, while in my head, I repeated, *Move on, please. Ask someone else.*

But he didn't move on. Kirk would not accept my answer. He simply said, "I won't accept 'I don't know.'" Then, he silently looked at me. And he just kept looking. I stammered. I repeated my original answer.

"But I really don't know." As I spoke, I got increasingly upset. How could he not understand that I truly didn't know? He wasn't being empathic or kind. My tears started to flow, and then my tears changed to sobs. I couldn't stop crying, and I wasn't even sure why. I only knew he'd touched some part of me that was so deep, so unacknowledged, that the dam within me broke.

All of my unspoken words toward my supervisor back at the psychiatric hospital came out in sobs. Later, I realized that they were, in part, about her. I was frustrated that she would not engage me personally or talk about the tension between us. There was no room in her model for vulnerability, which Kirk not only allowed but encouraged. Years and years of unspoken words would become safe with Kirk.

I later realized he would not accept "I don't know" because that was my way of deferring to someone else who knew for me. My place in the world as a woman with a strict religious upbringing had been to defer to someone else who *did* know the answer. Kirk would not accept that stance. During this first group, though, all I knew was that he had helped me break through the years of pain when "I don't know" was the safest answer. His refusal to accept my uncertainty was not harsh. It was loving and kind, and it placed value on my ability to know for myself because, in truth, I really did know.

From the first day I met Kirk, I committed to learning as much as possible about his therapy and supervision techniques. I wanted to learn to connect with people in the same way he had affirmed me. Twenty-five years later, through years of therapy, supervision, and, ultimately, a friendship with Kirk, I am a therapist today, which I would not have been without doing this work on myself. I probably would have chosen my second or third choice and gone into teaching or research. I am forever grateful for that first meeting and the ongoing relationship I've had with a person who has transformed my life and work.

My memory of Richard's first group is one of instantly being drawn to him. In that first meeting, I noticed Richard interacted with most of us but with just a few words. I cannot remember exactly what issue I brought up (most likely, it related to a client or a family member I struggled with at the time). His response consisted of a few provocative words (in psychoanalytic language I didn't fully understand) and then silence. The moment of quiet allowed me to absorb what he said. I discovered later that this was Richard's standard style. A few words, then quiet. During that first group, this method allowed me to decide how I wanted to handle his input. I was intrigued. I wanted to know more. Then, and only then, was he happy to talk further. His style struck me as both gracious and compassionate. His words had the flavor of being a gift, but he didn't insist on being heard or heeded. After that first group, I knew I wanted Richard to be a regular voice in my life.

—Lavonne

I feel that great trust and respect exist between the two leaders of the group. Clearly, they have worked together for a long time, and they respect each other's opinions and attitudes.

I see them as having different identities. I feel that Kirk always has a word of optimism and presents an opinion more centered on the here and now. Usually, he seems to take the lead in trying to say something to help unblock the group, while Richard is more meditative, trying to feel the unconscious communications of the group. He tries to speak to a more analytical hypothesis of understanding that is centered on the connection between past and present.

I particularly like this complementarity between them. Sometimes, I sincerely feel sorry for not being more fluent in English, as I am sure I would better understand the nuances in their communications, especially Richard's, whose communications are denser.

—Catarina

One of the most powerful aspects of TGC is watching Kirk and Richard co-facilitate. As co-leaders, Kirk and Richard consistently check in with each other and model how to be open and curious about a different point of view. They are willing to amend their perspectives as the process and the discussion unfold.

—April

For me, this group's structure has changed significantly in the last couple of years with the two of you leading. The experience has been emotionally smoother and more instructional. It has a better balance of group processing and teaching.

I had wondered how the group would change with two men leading. I find it has gone well. I don't have many strong, emotionally connected men in my life, aside from my husband and a couple of friends and peers. I appreciate the mixture of fathering, guiding, holding, and supporting this group has given me.

—Ann

I have always felt that the supervisors worked well with each other. I like to see them respectfully disagree or just have different opinions because it helps me feel safer, as they are able to be more authentic and model healthy differences.

—Randy

Principle 1: From Individual to Group Consultation/Supervision

Expanding Self-Knowledge and Experience, Alone and Together

A strength of TGC that I believe is unique from other supervision experiences has been the interpersonal experiencing and processing that take place among the group. TGC provides the opportunity to receive supervision on a case consult while simultaneously addressing the person of the therapist individually and interpersonally within the group. The experience of using the case consult to work on the person of the therapist (intrapsychically/psychodynamically) and interpersonally within the group is unique from my other supervision experiences.

—Laura, Michigan TGC

Developing Community, Generating Power

Consultation, whether individual or in groups, aims to foster therapists' ongoing professional development and continued growth and refinement of skills while contributing to the development of our field. Group consultation/supervision, and the TGC approach in particular, offers unique learning and therapeutic opportunities for therapists seeking to advance their clinical skills *and* self-understanding. This is especially true in TGC because the therapist, as an individual, is a major focus.

The practice of psychotherapy can be lonely with little opportunity to share experiences or receive any feedback from peers. Few therapists have a forum to present their work and receive feedback or have the opportunity to provide even informal supervision to a colleague in exchange.

When therapists feel unsupported in their professional questioning, either with difficult cases or their own emotional struggles, they can anticipate feelings of frustration, guilt, and shame, and a sense of loss will set in. The supervision that is most often available to help therapists sort through these feelings is individually focused on theory and practice. This may be necessary for licensing purposes, but the format may not be demanding enough; that is, TGC expectations require a greater commitment of effort and time.

Conversely, by allowing peer-to-peer interaction, group consultation/supervision opens multiple channels of communication. Most significantly in TGC groups, because the individuality of the therapist is a major orientation, lively and spirited discussions take place through authentic, open, honest, and respectful exchanges with peers. The ongoing, intimate nature of this cohesive collaboration offers members unique challenges and opportunities for self-knowledge and expression. Not only will therapeutic skills likely increase in such consultation/supervision, but individual members will also come to depend on an emotionally alive setting and a group of peers for assistance, support, confrontation, and direction. Especially vital to Richard, given his training in self psychology where empathy is such a cornerstone, is the therapist's opportunity "to not know" in a supportive situation. Rather than being professionally embarrassing or shameful, such a stance fosters a frank and honest exploration of countertransference, for example, which is so difficult to see in oneself or even in individual supervision. Kirk, on the other hand, benefiting from training in more confrontational models, is more likely to approach "not knowing" as a resistance and will respond in a challenging fashion. Often, the give and take of multiple interpersonal interactions is required to highlight the dynamics affecting or interfering with the successful treatment of patients.

We also encourage members to express any thoughts, feelings, fantasies, or fears regarding new members. We find such discussions particularly significant when multiple and/or conflicting professional or personal relationships are being considered. This invaluable input reinforces everyone's contractual expectations for honest and open communication about all major group experiences and interactions. We solicit various perspectives, and members' opinions inform decisions related to group inclusion. Consensus is necessary, and the ultimate responsibility remains with the group leaders.

Benefits of Therapeutic Group Consultation/Supervision

The benefits of this approach are multiple and address one of the most significant gaps in psychotherapy training—consideration of the therapist as a person with psychological and emotional needs. It is not only that TGC offers therapists the opportunity to explore themselves as whole people, but it is the way they can do this as a community that sets TGC apart. We believe this model is more comprehensive, impactful, and engaging while offering more breadth and depth than any other consultative or supervisory approach we are aware of. We provide the following examples to support this claim.

More Productive Group Interactions

Group interaction, especially in the TGC model, encourages lateral as well as hierarchical consultation/supervision, whereas individual supervision is unbalanced. In individual supervision, the supervisor has exclusive authority, an exclusive presumed knowledge base, and a prescribed role to provide assessment and judgment unfettered by the opinions or experiences of others. By contrast, the value of lateral, group member to group member interaction can generate less resistance. It is important to acknowledge that individual supervision can often stimulate the type of parental transference that interferes with autonomous, independent thinking and professional functioning. Unfortunately, compliance can impede critical thinking when the supervisor alone carries the voice of authority. In addition, assessment is spread out, with multiple voices having input on skill development, which creates a more supportive ambiance for self-exploration.

CLINICAL VIGNETTE: NICK[1]

Despite his large, muscular frame and infectious laugh, Nick all but disappeared once group sessions began. In interactions with others outside of the group, Nick displayed intelligence, wit, and kindness. He was articulate in expressing his ideas and genuine in conveying empathy for others, yet he would go silent and slide to the edges of the group once the co-leaders entered the room.

---

[1] In each Clinical Vignette, there are real therapists/group members who do exist, but each is hidden among various roles and personalities to protect confidentiality.

Over months and then years, group members tried various strategies to elicit his participation. They asked him questions directly about what he was thinking and feeling, joked with him, challenged him, and even pleaded with him to be more involved. Despite these efforts, Nick successfully frustrated members by his attempts to both engage and disengage at the same time. For example, he would make a point to bring himself into the group as it was ending by offering last-minute comments about what had transpired or by blurting out a sudden announcement when there was no time left to discuss it.

The group became aware of this pattern as it played out over the years, and it earned Nick the nickname "doorknob." Because this teasing was playful, the group offered him the recognition he needed in a form he could tolerate, which led him to feel like he belonged.

At times, others confronted Nick directly for what they experienced as his aloofness and emotional constriction. While his tone of voice could suggest support and encouragement, it also contained hints of harshness and impatience. The leaders instructed members to pay attention to and wonder with Nick about what led him to settle for so little interaction. Still, Nick would rarely offer more than a brief, wry exchange that left smiles rippling through the group at the end of a session.

Sometimes, the group grew impatient and threw more direct questions and comments at Nick, such as, "Nick, you've been quiet but not without feelings, I bet, right?" "Come on, man, give a little, will ya?" "Week after week, Nick, you play 'Come and find me.' Well, no more for me, Nick. There's no way you can play it safe and expect anyone to know you or give a shit about you."

Another group member who remained on the sidelines wondered why Nick so consistently violated the group contract about speaking openly and honestly to others. For his part, Nick rarely inquired about others in the room or offered spontaneous insights. In fact, when he did speak, he noted he could seldom see beyond his own needs and emotional reactions.

One day, Richard asked one of the group members how he felt about the way the group approached Nick. This member was on the other end of the sociability spectrum—rapidly talking to and about everyone in the room while excluding only himself. Though it wasn't planned, this intervention generated a heightened emotional exchange between the two members. Each felt judged and misunderstood by the other. As the interaction unfolded, more spontaneity, less caution, and more emotional contact developed. With the veil of niceness lifted, the group came alive with curiosity, empathy, honesty, and humor. The climate, though initially uncomfortable for Nick, turned out to produce some of the most meaningful and impactful subsequent sessions for him.

Nick was used to being ignored or passed over due to his parsimony and aloofness. Now, through the group's invitations, he could acknowledge his anxiety and experience emotions he couldn't on his own. Once the co-leaders brought Nick's proclivity for defensive silence to the group's attention, they would not let him disappear without checking on him. This was in marked contrast to his own family history and ran contrary to his tendency to become bored, sleepy, or resigned with his own patients.

This latter point was especially important for Nick's professional work. He had been perplexed, yet convinced, that his patients' many premature terminations of therapy occurred because of the population he treated. The fact that Nick's specialty was addiction disorders obscured the problem that he had trouble holding people in treatment. His reserved, hesitant demeanor, when combined with his detachment, could be perceived as a sense of superiority or a lack of interest. Perhaps even more concerning, his empathy bore characteristics of the academic type: distant, thin, and stiffly delivered. Through group interactions like the one we just described, Nick came to appreciate how his fundamental style of interpersonal relating affected him both socially and professionally.

Egalitarian Group Dynamics

The power differential is attenuated and authority dispersed in a group format. As a result, a real relationship is possible with the leader, one that is not restricted to transferential projections. This process bolsters confidence and proficiency by encouraging the thoughts and perceptions of all participants.

More Diversity and Options

TGC provides exposure to diversity in thought, perception, and ultimately in possible interventions to consider. Individual supervision options are restricted and limited to the information the supervisor provides and the discipline in which they have been trained, so other approaches might be given little serious study.

Trust, Respect, and Safety

Because participants have the flexibility to alternate between recipient and supervisor roles, the group provides a safe space built on mutual respect. The group, due to the number and diversity of participants, offers opportunities for experiential learning, including the demonstration of techniques where appropriate.

Enhanced Role Development

Participants can experiment with different forms of self-expression based on multiple roles in developing their professional identities. Wallin (2013) wrote that through attachment research, it has become clear that "we come to know ourselves as we are known by others, and our experience is created in our interactions with others." Attachment patterns are open to revision and change through the reality of such mutual, reciprocal influence(s).

Adding a new member to a TGC group, for instance, is different than adding members to a therapy group for several reasons. Because all group members are therapists, the current members might have a valid reason not to add a particular member. Adding a new person who is or has been a therapist with a current member may be a real reason for not adding them. Although introducing someone who is a friend or a practicing colleague of a current member will not likely be disruptive for the others, it may also be unwise for the balance of the group to have too many who are friends, members of the same practice, or who have a potentially problematic crossover relationship. For these and other reasons, we always announce the desire to add a new member and name the prospective person at least two weeks in advance of their anticipated joining so everyone can identify and discuss realistic objections. Group consensus is necessary for a new member to join. We expect that people will air and discuss any reasons for not accepting a new member. Our goal is to identify any realistic reason to deny a particular therapist an invitation to join.

Emotional Immediacy

The format of a group stimulates an immediacy of emotion, as a broad range of feelings is not only present, but also elicited (i.e., excitement, fear, anger, pride, etc.). Because the structure of individual supervision is restricted to one-on-one interactions, the scope is limited to the exclusive comfort and predilections of the supervisor.

Utilization of Regression

Regression is present yet modulated by the reality of the demands of group participation and the constraints of here-and-now exposure. Regression is sampled to assist trainees in facing countertransferential reactions, impasses, and enactments. Most significantly, group consultation/supervision provides the opportunity to focus on and assist with difficulties seen as central to the therapist as an individual. Group is a forum for experimentation and a laboratory for examining personal issues that may interfere with effective treatment.

Opportunity to Delve into Relational Styles

The process of group consultation/supervision provides the chance to observe and experience different relational styles in vivo. The push and pull of attachment is revealed in ongoing group interactions. Karen Horney's relational styles provide a context for identifying and understanding different modes of engaging with others. Horney (1950) identified three basic modes that we continue to find helpful: moving toward others (connections and accommodations), moving away from others (freedom and independence), and moving against others (dominance and superiority).

Group vs. Individual Growth

The group consultation/supervision leader(s) are able to use teachable moments to help all participants and not just the one presenting.

Affordability

The cost of using a group is significantly less than individual supervision. This provides many more students and young professionals the opportunity to continue and advance their learning.

Collaboration and Networking

A group offers a natural structure for professional community development; that is, a chance to provide and receive referrals, collaborate on professional projects, create co-leading opportunities among the members, and so on. McMillian and Chavis (1986) opine that a sense of group community has four distinguishing elements: Membership: 1) Members as part of a group establish trust to ensure emotional safety and a sense of belonging, 2) Influence: The more an individual is attracted to a group the more cohesion, communication, and participation will develop. Commitment is encouraged by those highly attracted to the group, 3) Integration and fulfillment of needs: The group offers support and allows each member to experience shared values, visions, and purpose with other group members, 4) Shared emotional connection: Members share similar experiences as they have individual contact. Caring and trust provide quality interactions and shared values in pursuit of a common goal or future

In keeping with the TGC format, we again ask the following questions: (1) What have you learned so far? (2) What has not been helpful so far? (3) How will you integrate what you just learned to improve your work and life? In our experience, these questions are best asked out loud, in writing to yourself, or to us at:
therapeuticgroupconsultation.com *or* **therapeuticconsultation.com**

In individual therapy, two people meet together to figure each other out, but only one gets paid.

Principle 2: Harnessing the Power of Group

Guiding Energy, Power, and Effect

I think when I talk about myself, about [my] shortcomings as a person and therapist, rather than simply talk about a case, I am receiving both educational and experiential feedback from the situation I am disclosing. This is very effective in my view.

—Ana, Portugal TGC

Provoking Mind-Full Collaboration

TGC is a unique model of consultation/supervision that provides experiential learning for professional therapists in a group setting. The therapist directly interacts with, is influenced by, and becomes emotionally invested in the group leaders as well as in other group members. The resulting group interaction centers on the honest, clear expression of thoughts, feelings, and experiences as they unfold in the immediacy of ongoing group exchanges.

Although theoretical formulations remain significant when we conceptualize the process of psychological change, the crucial variable for optimal group functioning is the sustained sense of immediacy and vitality in the room. Colloquially stated, we can say the moment of now is the reference point by which we determine and reveal effective group functioning. We formulate and apply group consultation/supervision techniques to take advantage of the multiplicity of opportunities that exist for intimacy and the countervailing resistances such vulnerability generates.

Sometimes, discussions can change rapidly in TGC groups. Seemingly benign information can trigger powerful, unanticipated reactions that had been lying mysteriously just below the surface.

CLINICAL VIGNETTE: KELLEY

Such a surprising turn occurred when Kelley grew more agitated and squirmed with some violence in her seat, only to suddenly announce: "I don't like who I am with her."

"Her? Who?" replied one of the other members.

While listening to the others talk about the benefits of establishing a truly independent practice (as opposed to joining an existing practice for a monthly percentage), Kelley had become more conscious about how she spent her professional time and with whom. This was not the first time she had struggled with the issue of time. Kelley had stayed in her marriage too long, remained with friends who took advantage of her generosity, and persisted in business ventures where the prospects of any meaningful return had long ago faded from sight.

Yet this intransigence was not how Kelley often greeted difficult encounters. Self-doubts did arise, though, when someone challenged her thinking, especially if the other person evidenced any traces of dismissal or disdain. Kelley had a mother who not only believed "children should be seen and not heard," but also put it into practice with a vengeance. Her mother examined any act of Kelley's self-assertion with close, harsh scrutiny and usually found it "unnecessary," "overly dramatic," or "lacking in common sense."

Knowing some of this history from Kelley's more than 5 years in this group, members could lovingly but strongly and directly challenge Kelley.

"You are listening to your mother's voice again. Leave it. There are no answers there. Listen to yourself."

"Make some noise, Kelley. Let us know you are here, here. *Now, now,* Kelley." Members said the last few words with urgency and care. The volume and the directiveness were meant to provoke Kelley and help her engage with the bright, assertive person she is.

The group was partially right. Kelley felt herself to be trapped between the ancient words of her mother and the current barrage she was attempting to withstand from her patient. Her plaintive plea had begun to wreak recriminations: "I don't care enough to do what I should do!"; "What difference is any of this stuff going to make on anyone's life?"; and "Even if I wanted to, it's too late." What

Kelley needed was silence—respectful silence for her to talk out what was inside. She needed patience and time to regroup and think about what she was saying. After a few minutes, Kirk asked Kelley to look at the others to see how they were responding. Then, in the smiles and the receptive softness she saw on the faces of her trusted group members, Kelley found herself in the place she had never left— at least, not completely—a here and now where she was valued especially for, and not in spite of, her struggles.

The Group Contract

The group contract serves as the foundation to guide and inform well-functioning consultation/supervision groups. Ongoing interactions in these groups possess the following characteristics: members make emotional space for one another, talk is simple and emotionally alive, silences are considered nascent forms of communication, open risk-taking is encouraged and supported, powerful feelings are present, intimacy begets intimacy, efforts to respect and understand differences are expected, and emotional connections are routinely strengthened.

Ana: I think the group is very caring about the way feedback is presented, and it comes from a place of generosity of heart, more than from a place of fear on how 'negative' feedback may be received.

The paradoxical nature of the group contract is intended to elicit what is restricted. Although the expectation that members put all feelings, especially about others, into words is clear enough by definition, it is all but impossible to achieve. The purpose of the contract is to provide a context to reveal and study how group members erect resistances—usual modes of avoidance—to limit their self-exposure and the risk inherent in living in the present.

Resistances: Opportunities for Growth, Obstacles to Change

Ormont (1993) has identified three major group resistances to living in the present. Because this information is not easily available, we'll briefly review it here. Group members resist living in the present primarily by using past tense language to respond to events occurring in the room. Rather than using past experiences to provide a living history of personal struggles, they present repetitive, complaint-driven, and emotionally stagnant stories. The group member adopts the passive role of being a victim of history.

One approach to dealing with such resistances is for one of the co-leaders to bluntly and forcefully draw a contrast between them and the description of a past offending relationship. For example, if group members are lamenting their childhood mistreatment rather than exploring their current feelings, a leader might suggest, "How am I mistreating you right now?" This intervention focuses on the immediate present and addresses the contractual requirements that members must talk to others in the room in an emotionally open manner.

A second prominent resistance is for group members to live in and talk about the future, often to avoid unpleasant experiences in the room. Again, the members' language and use of future verb tenses indicate their avoidance. We can witness this in sentences that begin with: "I'm going to…" "I hope to…" "You can expect me to…" or "I am really going to start listening to you." When members rush to the future in these circumstances, it's a form of denial about their present relational difficulties. The task for the leaders and the group is to bring such avoidant members into immediate interactions where they express their feelings. We can see an offshoot of this futuristic talk in phrases such as: "Should you just…" "If I were to…" "If only you could say…" or "I want…" which signal an intention, not a feeling in the moment. Group leaders or members can help by emphasizing the future tense that appears in another member's words. They can also occasionally request the member to make a statement rather than ask a question to highlight their resistance.

The third resistance occurs when group members focus on their lives outside, rather than inside, the room. When interactions are immediate and emotionally alive, their past relational problems manifest, no matter how distorted. Group members experience, rather than simply hear about, behaviors or attitudes that have become sources of embarrassment or pain.

In other words, the shift to living in the group's immediate present produces an in vivo experience that allows the entire group to explore both meaning and feeling rather than being forced to rely on hearsay. In this way, history is being made, not merely reported, and full group participation is more likely to develop.

Techniques for Developing a Functional TGC Group Process

Bridging. The technical approach perhaps most associated with group consultation/supervision (and therapy) is known as *bridging*. The term refers to any technique designed to strengthen existing emotional connections between members or to develop connections that did not previously exist. Bridges serve to resolve blocks and resistances to group flow. The premise is that immediate and emotional talk will lead to the release of latent psychological energy to establish or maintain people's emotional connectedness and safety. In working toward full participation, bridging helps address the group's underlying cohesion as a strong group identity is being built.

One method of bridging is to use open-ended questions to one patient concerning their thoughts on how another member feels. For example, we ask, "What do you think _____ is actually feeling when she purses her lips?" A second common method of bridging is to use direct questioning. The objective here is to bridge a gap between two members while alerting the group to their prominent feelings. In doing so, members become students rather than potential adversaries.

For example, we might ask someone who offered a stinging rebuke to another: "Are you aware that _____ feels injured by what you just said?" Direct questioning helps form links that remain imprinted in the members' preconscious minds. A third bridging technique is to ask a third, unengaged member to comment on an interaction between two others. An example of such an exchange might be: "What feeling is _____ hiding from_____?"

Analyzing Countertransference. When we conduct effective group consultation/supervision, another particularly powerful technical approach consists of recognizing, understanding, and analyzing countertransference reactions. For our purposes, two major forms of countertransference are prevalent in groups: repetitive and objective.

Repetitive countertransference occurs when group leaders repeat the most significant story of their lives without alteration—there is little or no changing of the storyline or subjective interpretation. In consultation/supervision groups, the group leaders' perceptions and behavior are not based on what members are presenting but rather on their own formative past, which still haunts them. The group engenders unresolved feelings in the leader that are so deeply entrenched that resolution sometimes requires a co-leader with some measure of objectivity to guide the interaction. A telltale sign that such a countertransference reaction is holding sway presents when a leader directs unwarranted, extreme, or out-of-proportion emotional responses toward the group and/or the individual members.

In more intense encounters, leaders seek to repair their own past. In this case, the leaders' countertransference binds them to a reaction so prevalent that it may be described as overly generous, solicitous, or complementary and even spills over into life events outside the group, seemingly with the intent to rescue rather than explore.

A second common countertransference reaction is known as an *objective* or *historical* reaction. These can be very informative because they are common, ordinary, and natural and, as such, offer a platform to examine the in vivo responses they generate. This is particularly true if the group is experienced in identifying the subtleties and nuances just below the surface of group behavior. We can also call this objective form of countertransference *matched* because the leader feels what the group member describes feeling.

Individually Focused Techniques. Thus far, the techniques we've described have to do with either the group as a whole or a focus on group dynamics. At times, however, the behavior of an individual requires more direct engagement to dramatize a resistance, demonstrate a mode of intervention, provide a novel learning experience, increase self-awareness, enhance a personal sense of agency or facilitate emotional expression and arouse action.

The Storm That Blew Through and Didn't Stop. The session lasted 32 minutes. It was supposed to be 50, my usual session length. 32 minutes was all she could take of me—and I of her, I realized as she stormed out. Those tempestuous 32 minutes made up my entire history with Sharon. I had never seen her before, and I have not seen or heard from her in the years that have since passed.[2]

The session did not begin well. Sharon thanked me for seeing her, saying she knew how busy I must be, and said she was honored to be seeing an expert in trauma, although she doubted whether I had ever heard a story as gruesome as hers. She delivered all of this at a rate of speed that left her words running up, on, and over one another. The rest of her was very still; not a muscle moved once she sat in my office chair.

---

[2] The original version was published in *Theaters of Trauma: Special Edition*, by R. Raubolt, 2012, Chapbook Press.

I suddenly noticed her eyes seemed to grow larger with each phrase or sentence she uttered. *A deer still in daylight but caught in imaginary headlights,* I thought.

Sharon's history, at least what I could catch of it, was filled with neglect, a number of hospitalizations, and, as she vehemently noted, "gross mistreatment by shrinks."

Well, what have I here? And why me? To whom was I a trauma expert, and why was this recounting of her "worst you've ever heard" history spewed on me within a minute of our first meeting?

Before I could identify any other thoughts, Sharon trained her jagged attention on me. "How do you see the connection—if you do, but maybe you don't, which might be good or might be bad for me—that is, between mania and depression?"

I said her question was complicated and said with such speed that I wasn't at all sure I understood what she was asking. I suggested she slow down a little and let me catch up so I could try to answer her.

She repeated her question, I think in much the same manner, if not more rapidly, while glaring at me.

"Okay. I'll try to answer the best I can because this question is obviously of great importance to you. I think you are asking my thoughts about what many call *bipolar disorder*—" That was as far as I got.

I was told I was speaking too slowly, and besides, "The real question is how you see mania and creativity because, you know, I am a very talented filmmaker—or will be as soon as I get the financing to make a documentary on my life. Oh, what a story—not a story, truth, a docutruth. That's what it is. Are you keeping up, or do I have to explain everything? So, what's your answer?"

I wasn't even sure what the question was, and my face must have revealed this thought, for Sharon abruptly and emphatically stated, "You can't help me."

She believed I was intellectualizing for my own benefit and using her. I stole a glance at the clock. Five minutes had passed, and I had spoken only a mouthful of words, yet I was intellectualizing. How would she know, when I had so few organized thoughts I could even recognize?

I tried to slow the session down somewhat and titrate her intensity, but this only generated more volatility and accusations that I just wanted to use her to buy a bigger home or boat.

Testily, I told her she was making a number of assumptions about me and seemed to be more interested in provoking a fight than in hearing what I might have to say.

Another emotional outburst ensued, and she told me she couldn't work with me because I was too into myself and my office was "all wrong, not good" for her. Then, surprisingly, she asked for a referral, although earlier, she had told me she had two interview appointments set up.

Still trying to salvage what I could of this session, I asked her to clarify what she was looking for in a therapist. What kind of person might be helpful to her?

To these questions, she fired off another barrage, but by then, I wasn't listening. She was beyond me. I knew no way to reach her, doubted whether anyone did, and I just wanted her to go away—quietly, if possible.

The quiet part was not to be. I wouldn't give her the name of a therapist to help her, and I told her as much, perhaps too directly. I had no idea how to speak to her. "I can't refer you to anyone I know because I don't think you would be willing or able to work with anyone. When disappointed, you fly into a rage, trying to destroy the very process you came here seeking. At least, that is what has happened with me."

Sharon stood up, pointed her finger at me, and screamed, "You are wicked, Dr. Raubolt. You are a wicked man." She wheeled around with her words still hanging in the air and slammed the door. 32 minutes.

I sat in my chair for a moment, took a few deep breaths, and called my wife to hear a friendly voice.

A month later, I was talking to a friend about ideas for this book and mentioned what was supposed to be my working title for this entry: "The Storm That Blew Through."

She asked simply, "And how long have you thought about her?"

It has been much longer than 32 minutes. Sharon had shaken me up and raised doubts in me about what I had done. I realized I was blaming myself and preparing an explanation for anyone who would listen. I told my story to colleagues and elicited their opinions. They assured me I had done nothing wrong and empathized with my questioning and worry.

I came to realize I had been turned into her abuser. Knowing of my reputation, Sharon set out to turn me against her, confirming her belief that no one could be trusted. In this one-act play, I was assigned the starring role that demonstrated to her that her fears, suspicions, and rage were much-needed props. She was beyond help, as I confirmed for her, and my wickedness meant she was also beyond redemption.

I was shaken by the experience. Yet, I doubt Sharon felt that way. She was, after all, the writer and director of this powerful replay. I can only guess how many times she has played out this defining act, but I am quite certain there will be many more, maybe just not so brief.

CLINICAL VIGNETTE: THE STORM, PART TWO — A WOMAN UNDER THE INFLUENCE

Kirk and I were leading a TGC where the group members began to discuss difficult, theoretically complex, and emotionally challenging patients, yet the members nevertheless spoke with little affect, spontaneity, or curiosity. It was if a gray curtain had descended on the group reflecting the degree of confusion and helplessness experienced in the face of severe pathology.

The whole group seemed to be experiencing an unspoken but deadly impasse: they were too anxious to proceed but too anxious to retreat. They seemed frozen in niceties, and the usual interventions that previously worked to encourage bridging or explore resistance were not having much effect.

In a conversation with Kirk after a particularly tentative and flat TGC meeting, we decided to provide an experience to indirectly challenge people's resistance. Rather than interpret, we used clinical material from Richard's book, *Theaters of Trauma*, specifically the story "The Storm That Blew Through."

A few minutes before the session began, Richard chose Mac to read and role-play the part of the patient in the designated playlet while he took the narrator/therapist role. After the group members were seated, Richard stepped out of the room to prep Mac. Once familiar with the basic outline, she was instructed to allow herself to become a woman under the influence (Mac was enough of a film buff to know the reference to Cassavetes's film). Soon after, she burst into the room, and for the next fifteen minutes, Mac became the highly resistant, agitated, and acutely paranoid patient depicted in the story.

Both of us played our parts well, leading to a more in-depth, free-flowing, and intensive discussion of severe pathology, paranoid projections, functional qualities of

resistance, and, particularly, projective identification. Acting the role of this patient helped Mac develop an inside-out feel for her fear of psychosis, as well as a taste of what it is like to feel so out of control and enraged that one's ability to function collapses and one's reasoning becomes elusive.

At times, we've found gestalt therapy techniques to be very useful; for example, double-chair work, confrontation and challenge, repetition and exaggeration of symptoms, as well as heightened focus on the nonverbal expression of blocked-off emotions.

An example may prove helpful: A young therapist beginning her private practice found herself discouraged at the paltry number of referrals she was receiving. When asked what she was doing to help herself, she responded, "Waiting." As she answered, her breathing became shallow and her eyes moist, so she was encouraged to follow her feelings. Then, a split was revealed between her long-held quiet, passive responses to uncertainty and the anger beginning to burn about her always coming up short. The division of passivity and action was represented by separate facing chairs, which she occupied when feeling one emotion or the other. Her movement between these double chairs helped her clarify her plans. Using the group as a starting point, she directly requested their help and referrals.

Many techniques are available for use in group consultation/supervision. We have presented some here and will discuss others as we proceed. At this juncture, one more technique is worth noting as an intervention that reflects an important attitude. The group leader in the TGC approach needs to feel comfortable with judicious self-disclosure that helps highlight the universality of certain dynamics, regulate emotional expressiveness, and provide a needed democratic stance. I (RR) refer to this as "leveling" which is conceptually equivalent to what Barsness (2018) has termed "courageous speech/disciplined spontaneity" defined as "speaking boldly to foster authentic interaction." (p181) On certain occasions, it is useful for the leader(s) to go first or go deeper. They might tell a personal story, reflect on a similar question about life's conundrums, and most significantly, express emotions that reveal a shared humanity so that positive healing attachments develop. At these times, the boundary between leader and group member is temporarily permeable.

CLINICAL VIGNETTE: GRETCHEN

Gretchen works primarily as a family therapist and as such, she hesitantly asked for time to explore a personal issue. While not immediately linked to her clinical work, Gretchen stated it was tied to marital/family issues in general. She then began exploring whether/when she SHOULD talk to the woman her ex-partner was planning on marrying, a woman who had been critical of Gretchen in front of her children, going so far as to accuse her of causing harm to her ex-husband. Gretchen's primary stated reason to meet the new wife seemed to be to help her children in adjusting to this new wife and her children. Eventually, Gretchen was asked to identify any reasons not to meet the new wife and her quick response was, "I don't want to," stated with some force. She quickly retreated from the energy of this forceful tone, stating that this seemed selfish to her. Members encouraged her to temporarily put aside these feelings and practice saying with evenness, "I don't wanna." This exercise was suggested to counteract collapse into self-recriminations for being too forceful, loud, and "prideful."

Hearing this last comment led Kirk to begin to describe the upbringing he thought she had; one steeped in tradition and belief in the sinful and underserving nature of "man." Such church teachings were particularly inhibiting to women, but all believers were expected to be modest, quiet, and subservient. He acknowledged this was his tradition as well, so he understood the struggles elicited by self-assertion. Kirk concluded by saying that he still hears the echoes of these principles even as he had parted ways with the church of his youth. Only then did he question Gretchen's motives for retreating into a more compliant stance. A lack of assertiveness had been an issue Gretchen faced before. The group on a few occasions pointed out how her lack of directness created money problems and frequent last-minute appointment cancellations. Her patients knew they would not be held accountable on either score. In this group session, Gretchen, sensing she had an ally in Kirk, began to reveal her wish and concurrent fear to think more of and for herself.

Expression of strong, aggressive feelings were threatening to her self-image. Kirk, sensing this, intervened forcefully to challenge her retreat. Most notably, he raised the volume of his voice and used a few profanities. These words were not intended nor were they received as dismissive or demeaning. It was clear to me; he was siding with her fledgling attempts to express her anger and frustration. Yet, I was not sure Gretchen understood what Kirk was saying or why. I asked her what she made of Kirk's responses, specifically the forcefulness of his language, which was very unusual for him in this context. Gretchen was able to see Kirk was attempting to "build a foundation of support." I pointed out Kirk was "lending" her a more aggressive tone and language she could try on. Group members were attentive and respectfully silent, giving Gretchen the time and space to express her hurt and anger with clarity and strength.

The group session concluded with a discussion of how and where a therapist's self-disclosure may be necessary to open pathways not yet available to a patient, thereby serving as a guide.

In keeping with the TGC format, we ask the following questions: (1) What have you learned so far? (2) What has not been helpful so far? (3) How will you integrate what you just learned to improve your work and life? In our experience, these questions are best asked out loud, in writing to yourself, or to us at:

therapeuticgroupconsultation.com *or* **therapeuticconsultation.com**

In group therapy, members help members, but only the leaders are paid.

By contrast, in group consultation, therapists help therapists, but again, only the leaders are paid.

In this emotional climate, our relationship with power and authority comes to the forefront. There is a very authoritarian approach that states a right and wrong way to do things. By contrast, there is a more laisse faire approach where anything goes and there is little safety or structure. Finally, there is also a more democratic use of authority where one knows what you stand for as a separate being and can respect the boundaries of others and their differences.

—Arthur Robbins

Principle 3: The Group Contract

Maintaining Promises, Honoring Commitments

One of the rewarding experiences with TGC is the fact it feels as if the group is building, throughout the sessions, its dynamics and identity. The group contract was sufficiently open to allow this.

—Rita, Portugal TGC

Tightening Flexible Boundaries

Some of the power of the group process is created by the influence, support, and challenging that occurs among the group members directed toward each other. The second part of this process is the developing of the skills of listening to and receiving of feedback from other group members. The potential for distortion, sometimes called "group think," can be magnified and observed among the group members. The power to influence, support, challenge, or distort infuses some of the latent potentialities of groups for both leaders and group members. Conversely, Freud wrote of the destructive, regressive undercurrents operating in groups (Freud, 1921). We can witness these at just about any Premier League soccer match or political rally and hear it in the unseemly chants so prevalent in college football stadiums. We see a weakening of propriety and individual conscience as the self is surrendered to the instinctual fever of the group. Harnessing the inherent group mechanisms for learning and therapeutic experiencing requires the formal structure of a group contract.

The Group Contract: Providing Safety, Creating Informed Consent, and Building the Framework for Optimal Group Functioning

This contract prescribes expectations for group participation and formalizes how safety will be developed in a group context.

Confidentiality, as we have seen, is the first requirement. Unless members are in charge of what they disclose and to whom, discussion will remain stilted and on a superficially polite level. We can anticipate few members will take emotional risks.

The central purpose of the TGC contract is to give shape to members' expectations and requirements, and, as such, it should be specific and detailed.

This specificity provides informed consent because each member, as well as the co-leader, clearly understands the parameters and rules that guide group behavior.

Contractual Agreements: Rules of Conduct

Rules for group consultation/supervision include regular attendance and the agreement to stay for the length of each group session, to pay group fees consistently and on time, to refrain from "acting in"—strong emotions are welcomed but must be put into words, not spontaneously acted upon—and to avoid extra-group contact unless identified ahead of time or structured. Real, outside-of-group relationships are fraught with threats of splitting, secrecy, and unholy alliances. Premature terminations are disruptive and, as such, should be curtailed if possible. As a result, members announce their plans to leave over a three-session termination. This process offers people the opportunity for a thoughtfully considered exit, which is beneficial to the individual member and the group. Group members are also encouraged to express any thoughts, feelings, or fantasies regarding the addition of new members.

CLINICAL VIGNETTE: FELICITY

We were waiting on Felicity to make her appearance for her last group meeting. She had gone back and forth for months in making this decision, saying she felt herself in conflict between her TGC experience and the training she was receiving in EMDR.

As is the expectation and part of the group contract, Felicity agreed to attend three sessions following the announcement she was leaving. This was to be her third and last meeting. As we waited for her arrival, and the minutes slowly ticked off the clock, I could feel my annoyance growing. Where was she? Why the delay? Why no phone call alerting us, a group of people she claimed to value?

Because group sessions were conducted over Zoom, Kirk was monitoring the comings and goings as people settled in. He kept an eye out for Felicity but to no avail. After waiting for 10–15 minutes, he sent her a note, one that sounded solicitous—overly so, to my ears—as he read it aloud. It also contained an invitation and possessed more than a hint of warm, forgiving empathy.

Reviewing Felicity's commitment to the group, I was again struck by what I recalled as her self-serving description of her EMDR training. This training offered her what TGC did not, although she was always elusive when describing how this could be so. Perhaps not as surprisingly, the interventions she described in her EMDR training were pronounced to be far superior to those used in TGC— gentler, kinder, unfailingly positive, and supportive. Felicity did not like to be challenged, confronted, or held accountable by her peers. She could be elusive, critical, and dismissive with others when they tried to offer her understanding, clarification, and support as she sorted out her reasons about whether to continue in TGC or leave. After months of such interactions, Felicity decided to leave by giving herself a self-imposed date to force the issue.

And still, we waited for her to come. When Kirk announced he had sent Felicity a note encouraging her to come, even if late, I challenged him openly. I said I would not have sent it, and in my opinion, it was a mistake. My reasoning was that she knew the expectations and the format for leaving the group. She didn't need preferential treatment; in other words, this was not something we offered to others who had left. Most significantly, though, I thought Felicity was being manipulative, or as I told Kirk, "You're making accommodations for Felicity that you wouldn't make for other members without indicating why this special treatment is necessary." I went on to suggest tersely, "She'll ignore you or present an excuse, but she won't be back." Silence enveloped the group as members nervously shifted in their chairs and focused their eyes on me, then on Kirk, back to me, and then to the floor. This was the most open, hard-edged disagreement they had witnessed between us.

Kirk responded just as firmly, leading off with, "You and I don't see this the same way. I think you're being too harsh, demanding, and impatient. I prefer to give her the benefit of the doubt, for her sake and that of the group. Some genuinely want to wish her well as part of their goodbyes."

We went back and forth, sharing our thoughts and feelings for a few minutes as we publicly sorted out our differences before asking the group to weigh in on what they saw, felt, and thought about Felicity, Kirk, or me in this exchange.

Their responses surprised us. First, they were thankful they were able to witness such a powerful exchange where disagreements were real (not therapeutically manufactured) and strongly held but where mutual respect never wavered. And it was true—we could challenge each other because of, and not in spite of, the mutual respect we had for each other. This respect is founded on the belief that our TGC co-leadership requires honesty, openness, and trust, as expressed in the contractual agreement. We have to notify each other about significant changes, positive or troubling, in our respective lives. (See "Principle 2: Harnessing the Power of Group.") Knowing what each of us may be wrestling with, for example, helps inform our decisions about who will take which role in a consultation session.

Beyond that, however, this exchange between leaders revealed that each of us believed in our ideas and was willing to defend them with vigor. Because this was also an opportunity for teaching and learning, we demonstrated the recognition that conflicts could be viewed from a number of perspectives. A key measure we wanted to underscore was how both personal experiences and professional reasoning could be presented for any intervention or interaction without damaging people's relationships.

Contractual Agreements: Guidelines for Effective Group Participation and Functioning

In addition to the rules, TGC has guidelines that define the most helpful attitudes and behaviors for people to offer in order to get the most from the group format. These include the following: each member is expected to take an approximately equal amount of talking time during the course of their participation; to seek to understand one another and put this understanding into words; to avoid personal attacks; to hold one another accountable for abiding by the contract; to demonstrate a willingness to engage emotionally with the group as a whole and help others do the same; and to voice fears and concerns about the group to the leaders. The golden thread running through the rules and guidelines is the willingness to talk about all important life areas that affect members' clinical work, including their past, present, and future. Group consultation/supervision provides a live demonstration of social problems due to the exclusive focus on relationships.

It is not expected, and experience has confirmed, that the group contract will be flawlessly adhered to, even during periods of optimal group functioning. The group, by nature, is changeable, volatile, and quite often unpredictable. Regressive pulls operating on individual members can be powerful and often fueled by the mystery of unconscious coloration. The knowledgeable group therapist does not expect members to be able to live up to the terms of the contract; they expect and are prepared for resistance and deviation. The co-leader is aware of the inevitability of individual, subgroup, and group resistance and of the probability of the deviant member being the instrument of and spokesperson for the resistance of the group.

Bion's (1961) work on the two aspects of group behavior—the "work group" and the "basic assumption group"—is especially relevant. The work group is the aspect of group functioning that has to do with the stated task and the achievement of its goals. Beneath this conscious level, the life of the group is entirely different, involving powerful unconscious needs that are embodied in members' basic assumptions about dependency, fight-flight, and pairing.

CLINICAL VIGNETTE: NORMA

Norma was one of the original members of the first consultation/supervision group. Before the group, she and her co-therapist were in bimonthly consultation/supervision with me. At some point, they ended their work together due to philosophical differences about doing group therapy. They never resolved these differences, and Norma decided to discontinue doing the groups with him and thus ended the consultation/supervision with me. She did, however, want to continue consultation/supervision, and at that point, three other therapists wanted to join.

Norma had been an active member for more than 25 years. Early in my relationship with her, she referred her husband to me, and he had been in individual therapy with me for 3 or 4 years. His therapy had been successful as he worked through a variety of relational issues. He ended "well," and, occasionally, we had some social contact, with at least one of those times being a social event for the

TGC group Norma was in. Contact between us at these events seemed friendly and appropriate.

Four years ago, my co-leader and I decided to end the group Norma was in. Many members were frequently missing, and it seemed the group was dying. We thought the group would not object, but to our surprise, they did quite strongly, Norma being the most vocal. She said the group was a very important place for her to talk about issues in both her professional and personal life. She committed to being more attentive to her sporadic absenteeism.

Looking back, I realize we may have failed to thoroughly talk through what was going on between the leaders, among the members, within each member, and between the members and the leaders. My co-leader and I failed to adequately address both the issues underlying members' absenteeism and what we acted out by suggesting we end the group. We failed to acknowledge the issues between us and with the group. Three years ago, my co-leader retired, and Richard joined the group as the new co-leader.

Because of COVID-19, we moved the group to Zoom meetings. During our fourth meeting, Norma sent an email to me saying Zoom was energy-draining, and although she did not exactly understand why, she had decided to end her involvement with the group. The other group members and I felt shocked at this— even more so at the manner in which she ended it, abruptly and with no discussion.

After 25 years with Norma, and after seeing her husband in individual therapy for 3 or 4 years, I was more than shocked. I was confused, conflicted, and angry. I know my anger originated from hurt. I felt this to be a betrayal on many levels. She was breaking our agreement that any decision to leave the group would be discussed with everyone in at least two consecutive meetings. Furthermore, she had announced her leaving via email without even giving me a telephone call. I found it difficult to understand because she had seen many members leave during the 25 years she had participated. Sometimes, she challenged their decisions to end, saying things like, "You won't find another place to get what you're getting here."

We discussed how to respond, and as a group, we agreed I would send her an email inviting her to a discussion and at least an opportunity to say goodbye. Given that Norma had witnessed many members exiting both in the way the contract stipulated and on their own terms, we hoped giving her some time to think about her decision would be better than challenging her.

After four weeks passed and Norma still had not responded, I decided to ask for a return call, indicating that I wanted to see how she was doing, not that I was calling about the group. She had had a serious operation several years earlier, and I was concerned about her health and about our 30-plus-year relationship ending this way. We had a friendly conversation with no talk about the group as I had promised.

Neither I nor any group members have heard from her since her departure more than 10 months ago. I still have not decided whether to invite her back when Zoom meetings end. Richard and I will discuss it with everyone and thus offer members the opportunity to more fully understand the group contract, the importance of keeping it, and the vulnerability of being in this kind of group.

Contractual Agreements: TGC Focus on Resistance

Our analytic contractual approach to resistance embraces a number of essential principles. The primary goal, however, is to maintain a consistent focus on dealing with people's obstacles (resistances) to expressing hostile, aggressive, and negative feelings.

We anticipate and welcome resistance as an essential dynamic of group consultation/supervision, and we view it as valuable emotional communication about the person's life history. We study, explore, and resolve it through the use of the group contract rather than overcoming or breaking through resistance using threats, intimidation, or humiliation. Resistance resolution is preferably directed toward the group rather than toward the individual. Where we have a choice of dealing with libidinal or aggressive expressions, we approach aggression. Following these guidelines, group supervisors can help the members establish controls over impulsive patterns that have previously tyrannized them and interfered with the pursuit and achievement of their professional goals and gratification.

In keeping with the TGC format, we ask the following questions: (1) What have you learned so far? (2) What has not been helpful so far? (3) How will you integrate what you just learned to improve your work and life? In our experience, these questions are best asked out loud, in writing to yourself, or to us at:
therapeuticgroupconsultation.com *or* **therapeuticconsultation.com**

To feel today what one felt yesterday isn't to feel—it's to remember today what was felt yesterday, to be today's living corpse of what yesterday was loved and lost.

—Fernando Pessoa

Principle 4: Two Leaders

Exercising Nurturance and Direction, Taking Turns, Together and Alone

I have experienced an immense amount of safety due to the pacing and presence of both Kirk and Richard. The process never feels rushed. In fact, time almost seems to slow down when I participate in TGC. Kirk and Richard bring an immense amount of clinical experience to the process, but they both seem to also be grounded in a sense of meeting what arises, moment to moment, rather than offering simple, canned responses. I experience Kirk and Richard as grounded in their expertise, while also remaining open to the input and influence of others in the group.

—April, Michigan TGC

Testing Trust

Groups, as used for therapy or supervision, have long been under the direction of a single leader for a variety of reasons. A single leader is often used when a group has a specific focus, such as in a lecture or a training group where the presentation of information is highly valued and can be delivered in a relatively straightforward fashion. In addition, a group format that seeks to demonstrate and provide instruction on either theory or technique may require only one leader. Arguably, the same would be true if the focus was exclusively on the dynamics of a group. While it can be comforting in this particular approach to "share the heat" when negative transferences prevail, it is not crucial. With TGC, dual leadership, conversely, is critical to successfully elicit and work with transference/countertransference reactions within the group and achieve a balanced equilibrium of cognitive and experiential components.

An Exercise in Identifying Supervision Needs from a New Leader

After many years of leading two groups together, my co-leader decided to retire from all group work. Thus, I was left leading the groups by myself. Knowing the value of having two of us, I decided to develop an exercise for the group members aimed at getting them to think about which leadership qualities would be most beneficial for their professional and personal growth. I consulted with a colleague about how I could best do that, and I developed the following exercise for them to participate in.

First, I explained to the group that I wanted them to think about the qualities in a leader who would be most beneficial to them in their professional/personal growth. Then, I distributed a form with six qualities, including clarity of thinking, the quality of personal/emotional contact with the members, the quality of contact with themselves, clinical knowledge/skill, the ability to hear what is not said as well as what is said, and the skill of co-leading. On a one-to-five scale, members rated several potential leaders for the group. I also invited them to recommend therapists they believed to have qualities most beneficial to them.

Including the therapists I was already considering for the role, we identified a list of six candidates in total. Five of them expressed definite interest in co-leading the groups. I invited each candidate to participate in co-leading a group with me and asked the members to use the rating form to assess them. There was room for comments on the form, and the members were encouraged to identify their own needs and why each candidate would be good for them.

Unexpectedly, when I explained to the candidates that I'd asked the group members to assess how they thought each would best provide for their professional and personal needs, three dropped out. I was surprised this level of stress was enough for them to eliminate their candidacy. It seemed to me that this is the very thing we expect of all group members, that they talk about themselves and their work and receive, at times, some critical feedback, both positive and negative. Surprisingly, this had become an effective tool to eliminate those who were possibly anxious about revealing themselves. Two of the potential candidates who withdrew indicated that in looking over their schedules, they realized they would be too busy to take this on. Yet neither inquired about co-leading just one group, so I suspect their anxieties were also a factor.

Specific Advantages with Co-Leadership

- The number and variety of transferential moments with each of the leaders allow for greater depth and more balanced learning.
- An increased variety and number of treatment suggestions are available, as appropriate.

- Leaders experience the ease of teamwork because they don't have to rely on other group members in working with a provocative group member.

- Differing theoretical and leadership models allow for the demonstration and discussion of pertinent therapeutic issues.

- Leaders provide a forum to both contain and express valuable disagreements.

- Leaders can offer consultation to each other between group sessions regarding group events and make plans to address issues accordingly.

- During or after the session, each leader has an immediate opportunity to get feedback from the other co-leader.

- Each leader can intervene in the group process with or without stopping or being excessively disruptive (e.g., can interject humor).

- Co-leaders can interrupt or stop the process to redirect or meta-communicate. In this way, important clinical and ethical issues are more likely to be identified.

- The speed and accuracy of identifying significant issues for each member, as well as for the developing group, become part of the group process.

- If it is necessary for a leader to miss a session, the group meeting does not have to be canceled—as long as the other leader is present.

Criteria for Selecting a Co-Leader

How do co-leaders find each other? The temptation, of course, is to look to colleagues with whom we practice. Yet, even in longstanding relationships, unknown personality factors might make co-leadership taxing. For example, having an office next door to someone and discussing cases with relative ease is quite different from responding flexibly and responsively in a group that demonstrates aggression by refusing to talk…about anything.

Careful evaluation and attentive interviewing need to occur because a poor match between leaders can be disruptive and rife with conflicts that affect the esteem of each person. The resulting effects on the training group can be more harmful as evidenced by members' unremittent violation of the group contract, including prolonged unproductive silences, interactions colored by sarcasm, erratic attendance, and advice offered instead of inquiry. Most damaging, members may feel they must choose sides and swear allegiance to one leader over another.

We have composed the following list to narrow the focus and help with traits to consider in selecting a co-leader:

- Honest, open communication skills and a willingness to talk through disagreements.
- An emotional range that allows for the expression of feelings in a modulated fashion—direct but expansive.
- Healthy self-care so medical and emotional emergencies are contained, attendance is not affected, and there is congruency between what the leaders say and how they live in the world.
- A demonstrated ability to handle members' "hot" feelings directly without undue defensiveness, withdrawal, avoidance, or recrimination.
- A personal life that is relatively stable as demonstrated by the ability to realistically face, describe, contain, and work to resolve problems.
- Intellectual and theoretical curiosity as revealed in a willingness to explore ideas, concepts, and approaches that are new, challenging, and/or uncomfortable.
- An investment in personal growth that keeps emotional vitality and integrity alive, or, as Mike Eigen has observed, "One must work with oneself all life long."

- A practice model that is well articulated, psychologically sound, and consistent yet held lightly, serving to guide the understanding of complex clinical data.

- Ideally, an ability to explore theoretical differences between co-leaders. There is a unique richness to be had when individuals or group members witness and have the opportunity to question alternate ways of understanding or intervening in problem areas.

- Sufficient emotional maturity so that the co-leader does not use the group as an arena to work through unresolved personal issues or chronic countertransference. In this same vein, the co-leader's psychological maturity is crucial to mitigate against their acting out unconscious resentments, arrogance, and/or self-deceit.

- Attitudes and interpersonal interactions characterized by grace, thoughtfulness, and kindness as well as a willingness to stand up for oneself.

- The ability to tolerate conflict and regulate one's own emotions along with the capacity to reflect conceptually even in the midst of a therapeutic rupture. Negative feelings about the leaders or the functioning of the training group will inevitably emerge, and how the co-leader handles this determines the success or failure of the group.

The joint leadership approach of TGC requires a platform for honest, open, and intimate interaction. Contracts that are useful with group members (see Principle 3) are also mandated between the leaders. These agreements are best articulated and written out and, as such, become a part of each pre- and post-group discussion. Because TGC leadership involves so many varied interactions, when emotions are running high, group co-leaders need to be able to count on a solid, clear-headed commitment to each other.

Initially, communicating such expectations can unleash feelings of discomfort because co-leaders have no educational or professional precedent to follow. Additionally, this degree of complementary self-disclosure can be remarkably intimate. If the contract is structured with respect and seriousness of intent, co-leaders will be in agreement that any uncertainty or unresolved conflicts between them must not be allowed to intrude on the proper functioning of the training group.

We (RR and KB) have agreed to the following working contract between ourselves:

Group Leader Contract

—Anything we observe in our work together or outside that work that either of us believes could affect our work in a beneficial or detrimental way needs to be an item for discussion. This is not optional. It requires that we are both diligent in making sure we remain actively involved with each other in all significant ways, both professionally and personally.

—All income received from our work together will be split equally.

—In projects we work on together, we each will contribute roughly an equal effort.

—We will discuss any disagreements openly and respectfully, with the expected outcome being a mutually satisfactory resolution.

—We will hold all personal information in confidence unless we mutually agree upon the exceptions in advance.

—We agree to engage in a thorough discussion should either of us decide to withdraw from our work together, and we agree to undergo consultation with an outside professional if either of us desires that assistance.

To this contract we give our good names:

Richard Raubolt, Kirk Brink

In keeping with the TGC format, we ask the following questions: (1) What have you learned so far? (2) What has not been helpful so far? (3) How will you integrate what you just learned to improve your work and life? In our experience, these questions are best asked out loud, in writing to yourself, or to us at:

therapeuticgroupconsultation.com *or* **therapeuticconsultation.com**

Principle 5: Practicing Ethically, Practicing Effectively

Practicing with Integrity

TGC has held a good balance of this for me. Usually, when I discuss a case, at some point, my own family or origin issues come up, and my own projections and personality-based tendencies (for example, the need to do things right) can often impede my own self-trust and creativity in my work with patients. TGC has challenged these tendencies while supporting an alternative process that fosters my personal growth. I have found the cognitive and educational information that is integrated [into TGC] to be helpful because I am oriented that way—wanting my work with patients to be empirically supported and based in theory.

—Kristen, Michigan TGC

Ethical Responsibilities of the Leaders

The leaders have a responsibility to their profession as psychotherapists. They are responsible for helping to protect the integrity of the profession by challenging the quality of the training and the work of the group members. The leaders are responsible for introducing key concepts from the practice of psychotherapy that enhance the development and growth of the group members. The leaders need to assess the capacity of the members to treat a variety of patients. As a consequence, they must tailor their interventions to the developmental level of the group members, making sure they are qualified to conduct the treatment of the patient being discussed. The leaders must consider many factors in intervening, including the training, psychological health, skill level, cognitive ability, emotional maturity, and social skills of the TGC member. The leaders also attend to the personal attributes of the group members and help them examine their thoughts, feelings, behaviors, values, and beliefs.

In addition, the leaders must gear the interventions to the likely needs of the patient, not exclusively to those of the trainee. This is ideally performed by the leaders, other group members, and the treating therapists themselves. All these parties must pay attention to the patient's psychological health, cognitive abilities, social skills, and emotional maturity.

TGC leaders have the responsibility to reinforce, encourage, support, and monitor the ethical practices for all group members.

The TGC leader will take on many responsibilities of a group therapist, and as members work through problems in group, their patients will benefit as well. This includes being responsible for the general overall quality of the group and offering an ongoing assessment of the treatment being provided by group members. The leader does not conduct this oversight to the same incisive degree as therapy, but it is their responsibility nonetheless.

The TGC leader, in taking on these essential responsibilities, is guided by the International Association for Group Psychotherapy's (IAGP) Core Principles from the Code of Ethics and Professional Standards for Group Psychotherapy: Brief Ethical Guidelines. The guidelines for TGC are similar and are oriented toward a group of colleagues rather than a group of patients.

1. At all times, strive to do nothing that risks harming the patients or the members.

2. Ensure that members keep their personal and professional boundaries intact in all relations with their patients. Instruct and remind members to restrict financial arrangements with patients to payment for services, and caution them that sexual relations with patients are never appropriate.

3. Be open about the limits of all members', including the leaders' clinical skills, and refer patients for treatment in areas outside your ability to treat.

4. Show respect in all communications with colleagues, especially when their opinion differs from yours.

5. Encourage and promote collaboration and relationship building with those colleagues who are your co-therapists or with whom you must work closely to better serve your patients.

6. Continue to study and learn from your patients and your colleagues, always remembering the complexity of the task before you.

7. Challenge/confront each other if you hear breaches of confidentiality, which would include anything other than patients at risk of harming themselves or another person.

8. Respect the diversity and otherness of your patients' colleagues. Their worldview may differ greatly from your own.

9. Be aware of your obligation as a healer to the larger community, including the international community, and use your skills to promote understanding and conflict resolution whenever possible.

10. Be modest in realizing what you can achieve in your special role as psychotherapist, co-leader, and colleague. Never underestimate your power in the lives of others, and never exaggerate what you can do to help them.

11. Make an effort to treat patients with special needs and physical handicaps whenever possible.

12. Adhere to the values of honesty and the principles expressed in the Declaration of Human Rights of the United Nations.

13. Obtain informed consent when initiating scientific investigations with your patients as subjects.

14. Strive to be happy and joyful in your work. You work in a field that is like no other in its great responsibilities and its deep satisfactions.

CLINICAL VIGNETTE: HOMEWORK

A year after the declaration of COVID-19 as a pandemic, it remained the most frequent topic of TGC group discussions. As a large number of patients and therapists had contracted the virus, patients could talk easily about the topic, knowing the therapist was also living with some of the same stresses the pandemic had caused.

In a recent group meeting, Richard suggested some features of therapy needed to shift to allow for a more flexible therapeutic approach with pandemic concerns so we could more adequately offer triage, crisis management, and psychotherapy.

He suggested all three approaches may be required with many patients seeking therapy during a public health crisis. Triage offers immediate therapist-generated techniques to reduce feelings of panic, terror, or depersonalization brought on suddenly and with no history of such symptoms previously. Some of these are quite simple but effective: holding an ice cube in a bare hand or drinking very cold water to serve as a distraction and to lower blood pressure and quiet the CNS, for example. Crisis management, while less immediate or urgent, can include suggestions to lower anxiety symptoms like hyperventilation, free floating anxiety, or feelings of dread. These might include focused and directed breathing techniques or tapping on acupressure points like those used in Emotional Freedom approaches. With psychotherapy, often, a therapist may need to begin a session by helping a distressed patient prioritize topics for discussion and assisting them with finding the words to do so. Everybody has to make practical, potentially life-saving decisions about personal protection and has questions about what to do and how much effort to expend to reduce the potential spread of the virus.

By way of another example, there was a very active debate around how much to facilitate patient venting. In non-pandemic conditions, patient venting might be encouraged to assist a patient in safely and effectively releasing strong emotions. However, this is often used when strong emotions are building toward a person in the patient's life, like a boss, spouse, or friend. The therapist can usually assess whether there is any "real" danger to the patient in the relationship they are venting about. The debate arose over whether, under what conditions, and with which patients the venting technique could interfere with the patient's cognitive ability to assess real danger and when the patient might need help in making sound decisions in the midst of the stresses caused by the pandemic. The leaders needed to devote time outside the group, which was unusual, to plan strategies to help the members process their thoughts and feelings since they, too, were in the pandemic.

At other times, patients need help managing the fallout these new crises generate in their lives, their work, and their relationships. Patients dealing with the limitations created by this pandemic must make an extra effort to manage these areas. In TGC, therapists discuss the added stress of helping patients focus on the present when patients desire to simply vent about their feelings.

For the first time in a TGC session, we offered a homework assignment. We asked members to pay attention to the shifting of focus currently required of them between creative ways they could continue therapy and, at the same time, help patients manage a pandemic. We suggested that whatever our group might be able to develop could help other therapists facing the same situation. We concluded that describing what was happening in the therapy room and how they responded could be clinically useful for all of us. In many ways, this conflict was similar to physicians seeing a patient with a medical problem that could be treated in a predictable way, but now the physician had to consider delaying corrective treatment because it was a higher priority to get the patient well enough to leave the hospital to avoid the risk of becoming infected with COVID-19. To return to our field, we suggested these priorities: safety first, triage next, and then crisis management.

Members respond to each other in many ways that facilitate the consultation process, but they do not assume the full responsibilities of leading. Their responses include questioning, clarifying, challenging, confronting, understanding, and supporting everyone. The leaders encourage and support members' respectful, active consulting with one another. Skilled leaders also consult with each other, both within and outside the group.

___

Ethical Responsibilities of the Group Members

We have already touched upon some of these responsibilities. This section clarifies and further distinguishes the group members' responsibilities from those of the leaders.

Membership in TGC is voluntary. Thus, it is different from most formal supervision, which may be required for licensing or training. TGC focuses on the total development and well-being of the members in and beyond their clinical work. It is for their personal development, first, because through such development, they become better therapists. Sometimes, members may discuss their patients, their interactions with them, or their reactions to them. At those points, the consultation/supervision is both for the therapists and also for their patients. To some degree, the consultation/supervision work is always for both parties.

Because all members of the group are therapists, they will sometimes fill the role of co-leader and other times of group member. The leader may assist by promoting bridges between the group members to enhance their development of the ability to present their own lives and work and, at other times, to collaborate and assess the work of other group members. Group members have a responsibility to listen to and consider feedback from one another and the leaders. They should give relevant feedback to other members, including the leaders, about observations they make during meetings. Specifically, group members are expected to develop good "group manners," including an awareness of time and air space and consciousness of thoughts, feelings, and communications that help or hinder the group process.

Many similarities exist between consultation and supervision. Consultation is voluntary and focuses on the therapist as a person and less specifically on their clinical work. For example, in TGC, the discussion often begins with some clinical question, but attention may be directed fairly quickly to what is happening with the therapist, what they are thinking, feeling, or conflicted about, all of which may appear to have little to do with the patient.

Both TGC and group supervision involve an evaluative component, with supervision being more specific to evaluating the clinical work of the member and with TGC focusing on what might be more at work within the therapist that affects treatment.

Role of the Group Process

Irving Yalom identified "therapeutic factors" characteristic of group processes and interactions that occur in 11 distinctive and related ways. These are all relevant to the role of the group in TGC.

Description of Yalom's Therapeutic Factors

From Yalom's viewpoint, natural lines of cleavage divide the group therapeutic experience into 11 primary factors:

- Instillation of hope
- Universality
- Imparting of information
- Altruism
- The corrective recapitulation of the primary family group
- Development of socialization techniques
- Imitative behavior
- Interpersonal learning

- Group cohesiveness

- Catharsis

- Existential factors

The relative importance of each factor depends upon the focus of any particular group, the length of time the group has been together, and the personal characteristics of the members. TGC is primarily self-understanding and growth-oriented. Little research and study have been conducted on this type of group. Thus, very limited empirical evidence or research exists on its usefulness. Similarly, limited research and studies have been conducted with supervision groups. Regardless of the lack of empirical support for the effectiveness or usefulness of experiential groups such as TGC, there are many obvious benefits and some limitations.

Benefits include:

- economics of time, money, and expertise

- minimized dependence on just one other colleague for feedback and interaction

- opportunities for vicarious learning

- exposure to a broader range of patients

- greater quantity, quality, and diversity of feedback

- a more comprehensive picture of treatment

- more exposure to a variety of treatment techniques

- an opportunity for reality testing of the accuracy of self-perceptions

- an opportunity to identify and overcome false perceptions of self and others

- an opportunity to practice speaking openly about oneself

- an opportunity to improve listening skills regarding feedback about oneself received from others

- support for the elimination of self-defeating behaviors

- support and safety in making personal changes
- support in overcoming a variety of work anxieties

Limitations include:

- concerns about confidentiality
- concern that more skilled members of the group may not get as much of what they need
- possible reduction of the likelihood of needing individual attention
- concern that an overly assertive member may dominate group time
- concern that a minority faction may get too little of what they need
- insufficient time to address all of the clinical work needs of each member's caseload
- difficulty in achieving the best balance of homogeneity and heterogeneity for the clinical work of the members

Each member can best address most of these limitations by having weekly individual consultation and psychotherapy, ideally in both individual and group settings. A therapist getting weekly individual therapy, group therapy, individual supervision, and group supervision is the gold standard.

Many group phenomena can be potentially beneficial or detrimental, depending on how the group addresses them. For example, these include conflict, competition, scapegoating, pecking order, passive-aggressiveness, and defensiveness, all of which are likely to occur unconsciously. Furthermore, if the leaders do not address the group process effectively, issues such as competing to be the group leader's favorite or an unconscious collective designation of the weakest group member can have a detrimental effect on a member, as well as on the entire group and indirectly on their patients.

Over time, we have discovered that group size is less critical in TGC than in group therapy (or traditional group supervision). Since the focus is on the member, experiential attendance is less crucial than in usual group supervision, which is more instructional, and theoretical discussions can dominate. A smaller TGC group has a much less dramatic effect on lowering the energy of the group. In a TGC group, two members can generate sufficient energy to maintain a high level of intensity. This is less likely to occur in a small therapy group unless the group has been together a long time. The longer a TGC group meets, on the other hand, the greater the level of disclosure, as both knowledge and trust develop in both professional and personal realms. In TGC, group members appear to take advantage of the smaller group as an opportunity to get more for themselves in their work or their personal lives. Members may have less fear of self-exposure or taking too much of the group's time. The leaders may also take advantage of a smaller group by increasing their involvement. So, with fewer demands on their time, interventions become more tailored, and pacing allows these to unfold without the pressure of time. Thus, group attendance will have less of an impact on the energy generated in a smaller group.

While empirical research is beyond the scope of this work, a brief narrative questionnaire was sent to current and past members of the TGC group in which the current authors were also the leaders. The full questionnaire is duplicated in the appendix. For our purposes here, a few anecdotal trends are noteworthy in relation to group cohesiveness, expression of affect, and self-understanding—all of which correlate highly with the most valued characteristics of successful outpatient therapy groups.

In keeping with the TGC format, we ask the following questions: (1) What have you learned so far? (2) What has not been helpful so far? (3) How will you integrate what you just learned to improve your work and life? In our experience,

these questions are best asked out loud, in writing to yourself, or to us at:

therapeuticgroupconsultation.com *or* **therapeuticconsultation.com**

As a leader I function on many planes of consciousness. I may be poetic, spiritual, playful, and paradoxical. I can also be didactic. I am also sensitive to group dynamics. These states can emerge as a surprise and a form of excitement to both me and the group.

I work with opposites or by contrast, I mirror or play or offer transitional objects. This approach may not be for every therapist.

—Arthur Robbins

Principle 6: The Person of the Co-leader

Knowing Strengths, Accepting Limits, and Staying Sane

Previously, I've participated in leaderless consult groups, modality-specific consult groups, and licensure supervision groups. This group is different than those groups, mostly in the focus/questions that surround the therapist/members themselves. In other groups, I find the focus is on correctly implementing a modality, diagnosing/treatment planning for a client, or processing about clients in general. What feels different about the group to me is the space given to the therapists being human and investigating/being curious about their experiences with/of a client and of themselves. To me, it feels like both group members and leaders are more curious or attuned to the therapist's experience than what I've experienced in groups in the past.

—Steffanie, Michigan TGC

Activating Audacious Resilience

Group leadership requires experience in either group therapy or group supervision. Although it is not required, it is strongly recommended that leaders have experience as patients in group therapy. Often, the prospective co-leader will come to know the power of a group to expand or inhibit an individual's growth only by such participation. Through group therapy, members experience at a deep, visceral, and personal level the powerful undercurrents present that come to dominate group functioning.

Personal Characteristics of the Effective TGC Leader

Experienced therapists are the best leaders for participative groups. Groups should have years of experience—we recommend at least 5 years of clinical practice—to be able to calmly decide whether to intervene or wait. Co-leaders develop this level of reflective patience over time, and it cannot be hurried. In this model, the co-leader takes on the main responsibility and guides, supports, and invites co-supervising by members. Such a group demands a leader's flexibility and confidence in encouraging collaboration with members without losing focus or becoming lost in the undercurrents that stimulate competition between co-leaders. This competition can occur between the two leaders and/or among the group members. In addition, knowledge of group dynamics and comfort with uncertainty is often, but not always, found in leaders with significant group experience. They have come to know how groups function from the inside out.

Effective leaders are able to view group interaction in a form of slow motion. Theory cannot substitute for experience. This said, beginning group members often do better with an authoritative group, in which individual supervision is provided in a group context and where there is less exposure to fluctuating group dynamics.

Safe and effective group functioning also requires leaders to offer a range of elements, including emotional presence and sensitivity, knowledge offered in a well-paced manner and with humility, and valuing vulnerability as well as competence. Group leaders are required to recognize the contrast between overt simplicity and covert complexity. Through years of practice, we have witnessed how confused and threatened a group can feel when this element has gone unrecognized or been handled poorly. Group interaction can begin to feel disjointed and chaotic.

Group leaders need to know themselves well enough to recognize their countertransference proclivities. That is, where and under what circumstances are they vulnerable to responding with unwarranted anger, dismissal, withdrawal, overly solicitous patience, sexual stimulation, or anxiety and fear? The leader, if open enough, will feel all of these reactions, which, if modulated, can serve as guides to underlying dynamics that members have not yet articulated or that are out of the leader's awareness.

Group leaders need to possess the ability to stand in when a member or group becomes critical and demanding. Quite often, it is positive but uncomfortable for the leader when they are challenged and confronted. Although a co-leader can offer silent moral support or skilled and appropriate redirection, both leaders need internal calm and visible, external calm to absorb tough questions and harsh appraisals of their abilities before responding.

One example can serve as a warning: A female group co-leader was challenged for her impatience and condescending appraisals. She responded in a manner that justified the group member's observation when she retorted, "There is only room for one alpha female in this group." Fortunately, her co-leader told her this was an example of her unwarranted countertransference. Maintaining a settled, calm presence and some measure of courage, though necessary, is hard to come by and even harder to hold on to when one is under fire. Our advice to new leaders is this: don't attempt to run a supervision group until you develop the self-knowledge, resilience, and fortitude that will allow you to contain your feelings while responding in a way that patiently addresses the issues and moves interaction forward. Although these skills are hard to develop, it is both gratifying and immensely helpful when you experience them.

CLINICAL VIGNETTE: COVID-19

As the group began to assemble, murmurs suggested COVID-19 would be the opening topic…again, for what seemed like the 500th time. The virus remained stubbornly elusive but deadly. COVID-19 kept members meeting remotely, speaking in voices only slightly above whispers, and passively listening to scripted stories seemingly told many times over and heavily laden with complaints of fear, resignation, and isolation.

We were headed into another such discussion when I decided to speak to this issue from personal experience. Rather than continuing with how patients spoke to us about COVID-19 and how, in turn, we speak with them, I adopted a personal, intimate tone to describe my battle with this virus, which left me bedridden for a week with a "mild case." I disclosed how frightened I felt to receive the diagnosis and my struggle to accept the realization that I could not will away or diminish the symptoms.

I was conscious of the line drawn between judicious self-disclosure and countertransference enactments. I realized as well that I was not only describing facts and details of my illness but revealing my vulnerability. My voice was close to breaking at times. I wondered if I would be able to find the right emotional register to evoke a different type of discussion—one that increased members' personal engagement and led to group cohesion based on shared emotional disclosure.

I knew from experience that when I took emotional risks, Kirk would step back and give me the space I needed, so I was unconcerned about going too far or missing the impact of my words on others. I also knew I could count on him to read me. Working together over time, Kirk learned to attend to not only the content of my words but their expression as well. I knew from past encounters that he listened to my tone as well as the volume and pacing of my voice, the intensity of my emotional expression, and especially any hints of sarcasm. These were early indications I could be overreaching—that is, pushing too hard or being too irreverent in making a point.

I knew as well that if a member had a strong emotional reaction to my words that was regressive in nature, Kirk would respond and work with them. Even as I continued to speak, he could carry on a quiet dialogue almost off to the side. He might encourage members to talk about their reactions to what I was saying or how I came across to them. He might redirect their attention and discussion to cognitive considerations—"Why might Richard be revealing so much of himself today?"—or, more pointedly and directly, he might inquire about reactions that were banging around inside but hadn't made their way out yet, or those that were unwanted but experienced nonetheless.

On this date, Kirk's only direct comment to me was that since my illness, I seemed angrier with the current political administration. I took this as his assessment that I could go even further if I chose. With that in mind, I let my anger enter the room with more immediacy, and, while modulated therapeutically, I delivered my critiques with steely evenness and biting wit. I was not venting, and I was uninterested in engaging in any political machinations. My purpose was to counteract everyone's immobilizing feelings of helplessness by claiming a forceful voice of protest and, in doing so, to invite a different COVID-19 discussion—one where group members could feel more of their emotional range and become sensitive to the influence of these feelings on their patients.

TGC Leadership: Reintroducing Spontaneity, Playfulness, and Creativity

A leader's ability to be provocative, direct, and challenging, when titrated appropriately and offered with respect and well-timed humor, is extremely valuable, though seldom seen as necessary. The usual judgment by less experienced professional colleagues in training, if the topic is discussed at all, is that these qualities represent the intrusion of group therapy elements. Although caution and solid clinical judgment are indicated, such warnings reflect therapists' fear, which restricts the range of interactions often required in experiential group consultation/supervision. Therapists' fear may restrict their creativity to the point that they avoid timely, respectful provocation, even if clinical circumstances suggest it would be therapeutic. In addition, the group contract provides the structure to incorporate thoughtful risk-taking.

Because the approach we present is experiential, emotions—often strong ones—are present, but not to the exclusion of thinking. When a leader offers a clear and comprehensive understanding of clinical issues, this titrates group members' emotions, which, if left unchecked, can lead to fragmented and disruptive interactions. The leader also risks losing the opportunity to offer theoretical constructs when members are most likely to understand and appreciate the impact of various interventions. They are expected to be conversant with various theories and techniques and to call upon them, even in the midst of chaos only groups can create. As supervisors have explained to us over the years, "Carry your theories condensed enough to fit in your back pocket because you never know when you will need to quickly adapt."

Most leaders use techniques they have learned in conducting group therapy. One of us, KB, meditates when a group member begins to talk in order to notice what internal reactions he has while listening. He reflects on how his responses may be similar to what he experiences with other patients or perhaps in other relationships. Such a process leads him to feel present as he imagines what he himself may need to face and what a group member is avoiding or mismanaging in their own life.

RR offers a different route, focusing his attention on what is happening in the group or with individuals. In this vein, he looks for changes in speech patterns, idiosyncratic word usage, nonverbal cues, signs of avoiding or aligning with another member, and subgroup formation. In essence, he attends to the interactions of the group members, while KB attends to his own internal reactions. Crucially, the leaders need to use familiar methods to help assess, interact with, and respond to what is occurring and what the group needs in the moment.

Group techniques are personal for each leader while also being known or shared with the other. With co-leaders, differences in style and orientation have the potential to be very effective if communication between them remains open, noncompetitive, and respectful. If a foundation of mutual trust exists, the leaders may also express their differences in the group to highlight various interventions theoretically as well as to demonstrate self-disclosure. Because the use of self-disclosure is often misunderstood or frowned upon, especially by young counselors, when experienced leaders demonstrate its effectiveness, the impact can be quite useful. These differences, when coupled with collaboration, become part of the teaching by example necessary in group consultation/supervision.

Groups need the clinical acumen of the leaders to see beyond the obvious. This means the supervisor uses their diagnostic experience to offer an informal, working assessment, both of individuals and of the group as a whole. This attribute is particularly pertinent when supervisors decide on group composition. RR, while in training, was exposed to and guided by a simple but helpful formula: "Never put one of anything in a group." If there is only one different—and noticeably so— member, the risk of others scapegoating that person can become habitual. In a number of cases, consultation/supervision is truncated until the singled-out person leaves or is pushed out. Experienced supervisors seek to establish an appropriate balance of active and reflective, talkative and quiet, challenging and cooperative, and cognitive and emotional group members. A consultation/supervision group composed in this manner offers balance and resilience.

One additional issue requiring special attention and sensitivity is for leaders to determine whether any members have significant personal issues. If, for example, a member displays evidence of mental health struggles, the leaders need to be able to understand the dynamic underpinnings of these struggles. Perhaps most significant, the leaders must be able to recognize when psychological treatment is necessary for a group member as an adjunct to or replacement for group consultation/supervision. Experiential consultation/supervision has more emotional intensity than individual supervision because group members' needs and competing demands can produce competition or anxiety at a level too high for learning to take place if not carefully titrated. Finally, the focus and the contract are established to protect the threshold barrier between supervision and therapy as well as to reaffirm the necessary safety for group participation.

Because many group supervisors have experience in group therapy, often as part of their training, they tend to borrow both techniques and theories and apply them to group supervision. While this can provide a conceptual understanding of group dynamics, there are significant differences in goals. Supervision groups have the stated purpose of training and providing consultation for younger therapists entering the field. This stated aim requires supervisors to become aware of the latest research for minimizing potentially harmful effects.

For example, some recommendations that stem from this literature include helping group members learn and maintain good therapeutic relationships, demonstrate appropriate use(s) of empathy, assist in offering steps to prevent and repair toxic relational difficulties, and recognize why some therapists may be less effective or may produce more harmful effects than others. This teaching need not be didactic in a formal sense. During in vivo group experiences, members discuss patients they find troubling or struggle to understand and the techniques they might use when working with these patients. Through these discussions, members can benefit from the safety and sense of belonging that their peers offer. In this setting, leaders can also offer exposure to and can model ways of relating (and thinking) that allow for a personal and immediate platform for learning.

Consultations

Although TGC does not include the formal teaching of therapeutic principles as a primary objective, we introduce and elaborate on theoretical concepts and technical questions we believe are central in conducting therapy. We usually focus these teaching consultations on material that graduate training programs either neglect or dismiss. Our intent is to understand, experience, and consider various diverse methods of practice and not to instruct therapists in one exclusive model of therapy.

Such information usually grows out of group discussions and spontaneous requests for additional prompts. As such, we present this material informally, frequently in a conversational give-an- take in which questions are expected and anticipated. We also deliver this information over time with added sophistication and complexity so it meets the evolving clinical needs of group members.

At other times, we will introduce a consultation/supervision experience designed to stimulate and, on occasion, to provoke immediacy in confronting a challenging clinical issue. We don't announce these experiences ahead of time so we can maintain elements of novelty, surprise, vulnerability, and risk-taking, thus adding freshness and spontaneity to our group discussions. We believe one of the most important skills a therapist must learn is the ability to adapt quickly and effectively to sudden, dramatic, and unexpected shifts during the therapy hour. In the TGC model, we create opportunities to respond to such abrupt changes with the background support of emotionally alive, interested peers.

We created the following pertinent schemas, which are central to two consultations we held: "Neuromuscular Expression of Emotion" and "The Four Levels of Communication." A third example grew out of the immediacy of the moment and was fueled by a member's intense Cymbalta discontinuation symptoms.

CLINICAL VIGNETTE: NEURO-MUSCULAR EXPRESSION OF EMOTIONS

Starting with Wilhelm Reich's work with orgone energy in the early 20th century, then Alexander Lowen's bioenergetics, Charles Kelley's radix bodywork, dozens of schools of bodywork, and more recently, Bessel Van der Kolk's book *The Body Keeps the Score*, psychologists are paying more attention to the ways we store and express emotions.

Here is a fairly simple, useful way for us to understand how the eight main emotions are expressed and blocked. Borrowing from the original work of Reich and more recently from Kelley, developer of Radix body and author of *Life Force*, I described to the group the similarities between four major pairings of emotions: fear/trust, pain/joy, anger/love, and happiness/sadness. In the group, we were talking about fear, and I used that, plus the other pairings, to compare and contrast.

One muscular blockage of fear is located in the back of the neck. When we block fear, the muscles there tighten. When we freely express fear, they extend during an intense inhalation. These muscles literally pull the head back, allowing the lungs to fill with oxygen so we will be optimally prepared if danger approaches. We engage the vision intensely on the inside to prepare for fight, flight, or freeze responses. There is a certain kind of blindness at play. The "eyes" are looking inward for a moment to intensify "thoughts" as the fight/flight options are rifling through the mind. In bodywork terminology, this is called an "instroke," which also intensifies heartrate and other physical responses associated with fear.

We pair fear with trust. The blockage to the expressive release of fear displaces the opportunity for trust, which is the opposite of fear.

By way of contrast and comparison, I briefly discussed two other pairings. For the pain/joy pairing, we can easily relate to a situation wherein we block the urge to cry, perhaps because of a sense of social awkwardness. This, referred to as a lump in your throat, is the muscular block against the full expression and free release of the desired crying or even sobbing. Similarly, there are other levels of muscular blocking of which are referred to as "armoring the body".

We can also easily identify in our own bodies the anger/love pairing. We usually feel a blockage of anger coming up from the sides of the neck. The jaw clenches, and we feel the desire to head-butt the object of our anger. Unlike fear, which prepares us to consider more options, anger focuses us on primarily one thing: the object of our anger. A good example of this is a mother bear protecting her cub. The neuromuscular pairing with anger is love, in that there is often one object we are focused on. As the blockages to the full expression of anger soften, it permits the free flow of loving impulses and often the belief that this one object will satisfy the loving feeling, and thus we may pursue this object with a similar singularity of focus.

CLINICAL VIGNETTE: FOUR LEVELS OF COMMUNICATION

This section grew out of a discussion about how group therapy might be an important addition for therapists to use in treating their current patients. People made suggestions about using both modalities with a single patient or using only group therapy. We noted that group therapy offers a powerful method for patients to develop and practice four important levels of communication.

The first is for us to be able to speak about ourselves with the goal of saying what is truthful without holding back, downplaying, or exaggerating in any way. It is a chance for us to develop the skill of speaking about ourselves.

The second is for us to speak to others about things we observe in them that, in most situations, we might not say because of some emotional reason—most frequently, anxiety. This provides an opportunity for us to develop the skill of speaking the truth to others as best we see it in a clear and direct way.

The third is for us to practice and develop the kind of listening that is as free as possible from defensiveness as well as to make sure we fully understand what is being said to us about ourselves. At first, most people eliminate things that sound defensive, but with practice, we can learn to become emotionally open, inviting, and desirous of hearing this kind of information about ourselves.

The fourth is that we listen to make sure the other person has accurately heard what we have said, including what we did not say aloud but may have communicated nonverbally. We do this for the sake of clarifying whatever they may have missed or distorted. We learn to listen and insist we are heard and understood accurately.

These skills are not about getting others to agree with us or to convince them of something. Obviously, these skills can be promoted and developed in individual therapy, too, but group therapy provides a unique chance for us to get feedback from multiple sources as well as opportunities to interact with peers.

CLINICAL VIGNETTE: MCKENZIE

McKenzie sat with her feet tucked up and under her thighs. Her eyes were closed as she swayed to some disjointed rhythm known only to her. In contrast to her usual outgoing, witty attentiveness to others, today, "Mac" was distraught and withdrawn. Despite her discomfort, or perhaps because it was so acute, she began the group with a plea for help. As her story unfolded, the reasons for her agitation provided a personal learning experience for the group on the potentially dangerous side effects of coming off psychiatric medications.

About eight months earlier, Mac was prescribed Cymbalta for depression and physical pain following a number of family traumas. While this medication seemed to provide some relief, or at least coincided with the lessening of her symptoms, Mac maintained her anti-medication stance. She believed in diet, exercise, and meditation—natural ways to combat physical discomfort and disease. She experienced an uneasy tension between the emotional regulation the medication offered her and the sense of shame and disappointment she suffered from for responding favorably to the drugs. She had talked about this struggle in group a number of times, but the depth of this internal conflict was just beginning to surface.

In a burst of determination, she decided to inform her GP that she planned to wean herself off of Cymbalta. Mac read up on different ways to go about this and decided to stagger the amount she would take. One day, she would take a whole tablet, and the next day, half a tablet. For the first few days, this plan seemed to be working. Suddenly, however, she began to develop severe twitching in her eyes, tremors, agitation, insomnia, and loss of appetite, and feelings of depersonalization began to form. Her physician assured her it was temporary but, by either word or deed, implied she was overly sensitive. Feeding into her shame, she heard she was being "too emotional."

As Kirk and I began to unpack her story, we wanted to provide her with quiet patience, empathy for what she was going through, and greater clarity regarding the problem and how to address it. We began to explore the use of antidepressant medications, particularly the risk factors involved, their anticipated effectiveness, the length of time prescribed, side effects, and the recommended process to discontinue such medications. This session involved group interaction, but it was largely in response to what Kirk and I were structuring. From our initial starting point, the conversation evolved over the next 90 minutes.

As a group of non–medically trained therapists, most members were unaware of the risks present with antidepressant medications and with Cymbalta, in particular. We spent some time discussing these risks and helping Mac understand the effects of withdrawal. The drug's intense withdrawal symptoms have been designated "Cymbalta discontinuation syndrome," which includes severe mood swings and "brain zaps." This latter symptom is what Mac identified with headaches and the feeling of zaps of electricity often to her head, leaving her unable to function and in a state of panic.

We went into some detail in explaining that Cymbalta has a short half-life, or the time it takes the body to eliminate half the dosage. The shorter the half-life of a medication, the more frequent and severe the side effects. Cymbalta's half-life of 12 hours is exceedingly short. We cited research that suggests 40–50% of patients experience troublesome side effects when discontinuing, and 10% develop severe symptoms. To broaden the discussion, we also discussed studies that concluded antidepressant medication was superior to taking a placebo—but only slightly. The effectiveness of this category of medication is about 33%, which, as one psychiatrist I consult with noted, "would be unacceptable in any other branch of medicine."

As group members began to react, they were initially stunned and disturbed that this information was not more readily available. Not only were they interested in learning more for their own benefit, but they also voiced a desire to organize a clearinghouse, of sorts, to provide current information on psychiatric drugs of various kinds. Mac was relieved to know what caused the brain zaps she experienced. She also felt grateful for a referral to a social worker trained in the effects of psychiatric medication. Kirk and I insisted she would learn more and feel more confident if a plan were developed by an expert who also spoke to her lifestyle choices.

CODA

(AFTERWORD, EPILOGUE, POSTSCRIPT, EXCURSUS, CODICIL, DENOUEMENT, OH MY…)

May 1, 2021

Kirk,

I suggest we consider a different ending to our manual. We have received feedback from "TGC readers" pointing out that we moved away from the relational lessons we learned as we completed this writing. I agree. So, with that in mind, I have been trying to capture the right format for "our" ending. I am thinking of a coda, although I am open to other variations, i.e., codicil, excursus, etc., with slight nuances to express how our relationship was present from start to finish. A coda is my selection, though, because it allows for a meditative, reflective view of how we have written together.

I think we could, for example, start with a quote from Coimbra de Matos as an epigraph:

"Learning from experience, which means learning from mistakes—by trial and error. Hypothesis and proof; not only evidence and verification, but also refutation and falsification."

His quote quite beautifully describes our process in completing this manual and also the manner in which we have developed and practiced TGC—many starts and stops before we were able to find the right tone, pacing, words, and direction. We moved from a more academic, stiff articulation of our ideas to include a more personal and immediate feel. Hell, who starts a training manual with personal stories that are so disclosive in nature? Yet, this is where we found our footing and made this project of ours come alive emotionally. And it only took us some 40 years to figure this out. Quick studies, us?

Perhaps because I am in love with Portugal (and I expect you will be as well soon) and the deep simplicity of Coimbra's words, I suggest we return to him for a second epigraph—we can have as many as we wish. Anyway, in a personal exchange, he identified the three virtues of the analyst (therapist): patience, tolerance for doubt, and intellectual humility. These two epigraphs go together to describe us. The "us" who take chances, explore new options, keep ideas fluid and moving, all with a sense of wonder and confidence that "we can figure this out."

May 3, 2021

Kirk,

I suggested this format as a nice "wind-down" conclusion—personal, quiet, and reflective. I head off for a holiday weekend, confident we were going in the right direction, but oh no, you had other ideas. In my absence (I repeat, just two days!!), you take off, flooded with new ideas, formats, extensions, and God knows what else, which is to say you caught me flat-footed. Not that *your* coda is something I disagree with—how could I? It is an expression of your best writing, but you narrowed and selected a different approach so quickly. That has been my job, dear friend.

So now, finding myself batting second to your leadoff hitting, let's see what I can do with what you have done. Once more into the fray, not unlike how I find myself following you in our groups, I might add.

Here goes…
Edited Coda

KB Coda: (Richard's edits and comments in bold print)
This is not a traditional coda. I have been "Brinked," as TGC groups have designated your uncommon twists of mind. Still, I'll go with you.

Now that this manual is near completion, here are a few questions/**challenges:**

How shall I live with Richard?
Hell, how do we live with each other? You can't support me without expecting the same.

- Stand beside him and behind him in friendship as he and I work to improve the practice of psychotherapy and help those practicing psychotherapy.
- Encourage and join him *as we* respond to this second question.

How shall we live—*defined as engaging, challenging, enjoying, and playing*—with other therapists?

We shall live with other therapists by:

- Learning everything they have to teach us.

- Teaching them that what we believe is valuable for them to understand and practice. *Amen.*

- Teaching them how to emotionally hold others and how to be held.

- Facilitating and *expecting* them to seek wisdom and enlightenment.

- Encouraging them to be courageous, live responsibly, practice self-control, and seek justice.

- Guiding them to seek and find beauty and goodness in the world.

- Guiding them *to* recognize, *feel, and* practice gratitude.

- Helping them find their own peace, strength, willpower, self-respect, and spirit.

- Promoting and *directing* them to give back to their profession through their own efforts to teach, write, and energize professional practices of the highest quality.

- Insisting they think for themselves, attend to what is alive inside of them, and contribute to improving the practice of psychotherapy.

How shall we live with our mentors? *Aren't we doing this and with both humility and grace?*

- Honor them for what they have given to us.

- Give them deserved credit.

- Be grateful for what they taught, continue to teach, and what they have not taught us, forcing us to learn for ourselves.

How shall we treat our patients? *Now, wait a minute. Aren't you starting a new book here?*

- Treat them as we would want to be treated by our therapists.
- Face them with the truth.
- Stand in front, stand ahead, stand beside, and stand behind them as necessary.
- Confront, challenge, provoke, caution, and embrace them as necessary.
- Help them build courage, self-respect, self-control, wisdom, and peace.
- Help them seek justice and practice kindness and gratitude.
- Help them orient themselves to what is good, beautiful, and true.

And no sooner do I ask if you have a new book in mind than I receive an email suggesting we change the title of this manual by adding, "A Practical Guide to Becoming/Being a Psychotherapist." I shake my head with affection and wonder who else would suggest a title change in the coda. You will take the lead for this next one, my friend, and I will gratefully follow.

How shall I treat myself? *I will ask the same of/for myself.*

- Tell the truth always. *I give a little leeway here—the word "always" gives me pause.*
- Develop a receptivity and desire to hear and see the things I do not want to hear about myself.
- Work vigilantly at eliminating unconscious self-deceit. *Not all self-deceit is unconscious.*
- Live fully in the moment while attending to my direction in life.
- Choose the pain of self-discipline over the pain of regret and disappointment.
- Remain oriented to what is good and beautiful in the world.

- Live today. Do not spend time and energy regretting the past or being anxious about the future.

You are not what happens to you. You are what you choose to become (Carl Jung), or, in a more contemporary vein, Crosby, Nash, and Young remind us of this in a simple, clear rhyme:

You, who are on the road

Must have a code that you can live by

And so, become yourself

Because the past is just a goodbye.

This manual is ending, but it is not the end of our work together with the therapists in our TGC groups, or hopefully with you, the reader. We hope that this manual will be useful for you in ways similar *to how* the coda we have developed is useful to us.

TO ALL THERAPISTS:

Do not ignore your development as a person and as a therapist. Be grateful, savor it, embrace it, protect it, and get others to join you in that process. It will make your world and the worlds of others better.

Acknowledgments

The first person I wish to acknowledge is my co-author, Richard Raubolt. I met him in 1976 when he was doing his doctoral internship at a psychiatric hospital. I worked as a staff psychologist at that facility, and I was asked to do a presentation to the interns. Richard impressed me by being able to think critically and ask challenging questions. We remained colleagues but did not work together until the '90s when, as mentioned in "Kirk's Story," he invited me to a group supervision meeting. Consequently, we were members of this supervision group for most of that decade. It was his idea to write this manual. His experience of having written and published previously has been so very valuable in writing and completing this. He edited almost everything I contributed and, more importantly, doggedly persisted in the development and completion. He has similarly "edited" my work in the five groups—four TGC and one therapy group—we do together. I have a great deal of freedom knowing I can experiment in our groups because I am confident he will correct, add to, tag-team, challenge, clarify, and/or elaborate as necessary. Although I value his clinical skills, his friendship is what I treasure most.

I have sought out many group supervisions, consultations, and therapy experiences during my entire professional life. Currently, I co-lead 10 groups. I have also been a board member during the last 20-plus years of the Michigan Group Psychotherapy Society and the Institute of Individual and Group Psychotherapy. I have been in supervision and/or psychotherapy with Natan HarPaz, Reuven Bar-Levav, Ronald Hook, Paul Shultz, Charles Kelley, John Rierson, Pamela Torraco, Jim Stanislaw, Leora Bar-Levav, Marcia Stein, and David Baker. I have co-led weekly therapy groups with Richard Raubolt, Sheila McCormack, Mary Jo Drueke, John Weiks, Karen Wassink, Mary Bennett, Pat Hickey, and Sally Ryan. In addition to these, I have co-led extended groups with Natan HarPaz, Jim Stanislaw, Ronald Hook, Marcia Stein, Leora Bar-Levav, and John Rierson. I credit the work I do to these people and what they have given to me for my development, personally and professionally. Primarily, however, this book is based on what the therapist group members and my patients have taught me and have patiently helped me see, believe, and accept about myself and my work.

There are too many friends to name, but I want to name the members of one very important nonprofessional men's group. It includes Tom, Tim, Chuck, Aaron, Bill, John, and Richard and has met every other week for more than 30 years.

My oldest son, Brandon Brink, a graphic artist, has contributed to various aspects of the design of this manual, along with his considerable technical skills. My children, who are in the psychotherapy business—Aaron Brink, PsyD; Stacy Brink, PsyD; and Jon Brink, MSW—have offered ideas as well as encouragement.

Finally, Catharine Walstra, my loyal friend and partner, has provided the technical assistance and emotional support necessary for me to complete this project. Her love and inspiration are life sustaining for me.

—KB

Well, now we are again going to have some contrast. Because Kirk (and the reader, by now) knows how much love and respect I have for him, I want to acknowledge only one other major influence in my professional life, although there have been many. In my writing to date, I have failed to address my debt to him. This stops now. Dr. Thomas Bratter. Tom. "In the struggle together," just above his signature, closed his every letter for the 30 years I knew him. It was also his code for life— he was tough, his confrontations could be withering and his love boundless. From my first graduate days at Columbia, Tom taught me (although *forced* may be more descriptive, at least at times) to go beyond my feelings of comfort, to fight for what I believed in, and, if the cause was right, to bring all my resources to bear. And in the early 1970s, he showed me how to love my patients. In other words, he was ahead of the field by a good 40 years, but then again, he always played on the edges of professional respectability—pushing boundaries and questioning orthodoxy. I have tried to live and pass on "Bratter's" code, and although I do not have his brashness, I know how to acknowledge him: "Tom, I thank and miss you. I remain in the struggle together…always."

—RR

Appendix

Therapeutic Group Consultation Questionnaire

1. How does TGC compare with other forms of supervision you have experienced? Name some forms of supervision, and please identify their strengths and weaknesses compared with TGC.

2. How effective was TGC in integrating cognitive/educational information with experiential components? Give a personal experience if possible.

3. Did you ever feel as if your personal boundaries were not being respected and that pressure from the leaders or the group negatively affected your perceptions of yourself as a person or as a therapist? Explain.

4. Did you feel you could ask questions or state differences in thinking with the leaders and/or the group? Please give examples.

5. On a scale of one to five, with five being the highest, how safe did you feel to bring up a personal concern that was impinging upon your professional work? What were the factors that led to these positive or negative feelings about safety in TGC?

6. Were different theoretical models of practice given appropriate airtime for you to study, understand, and appreciate the relative strengths and weaknesses of each? Was this material that you were led to believe or thought would be included?

7. How actively did group members offer one another understanding and discussion of pertinent issues affecting the group; that is, attendance, participation, and so on? To what degree did members provide honest "here and now" feedback to you personally or professionally?

8. Did the group contract, as described, mirror the manner in which it was developed and utilized in your group?

9. Did you experience the leaders working effectively together, especially when intervening emotionally, teaching, presenting information, or developing treatment strategies? Were they forthright and respectful in their interactions with each other?

10. Name one area that the group leaders could improve on in offering this model of consultation/supervision.

ADDITIONAL QUESTIONS:

> What is an example of something that was particularly helpful in your group experience?
>
> What is an example of something that was not helpful or was mismanaged?
>
> What do you wish you had said or not said?
>
> What would improve this experience for you?
>
> How has your psychotherapy practice benefited by your being in this group?
>
> In which ways have you benefited personally?

—Richard Raubolt and Kirk Brink

References

American Psychological Association. (2013). Recognition of psychotherapy effectiveness: The APA resolution. *Psychotherapy, 50*(1).

Barsness, R. (2018). *Core competencies of relational psychoanalysis.* Routledge.

Bowlby, J. (1969). *Attachment and loss: Vol. 1. Attachment.* Basic Books.

Bowlby, J. (1988). *A secure base: Clinical applications of attachment theory.* Routledge.

Freud, S. (2001). *Group psychology and the analysis of the ego* (Ethel Spector Person, Ed.). Routledge. (Original work published 1921)

Hazanov, V. (2019). *Fear of doing nothing.* Sphinx Books.

Kaye, P. (2013). *Group therapy through the lens of attachment theory: An interview with David Wallin, PhD.* American Group Psychotherapy Association.

Kelley, C.R. (2004). *Life force…the creative process in man and in nature.* Trafford.

Marmarosh, C., Markin, R., and Spiegel, E. (2013). *Attachment in group psychotherapy.* American Psychological Association.

Marmarosh, C. (2014). Empirical research on attachment in group psychotherapy: Moving the field forward. *Psychotherapy*, *51*(1).

Marmarosh, C. (2015). Emphasizing the complexity of the relationship: The next decade of attachment-based psychotherapy research. *Psychotherapy*, *52*(1).

McMillan, P., and Chavis, D. (1986). Sense of community: A definition and theory. *Journal of Community Psychology, 14*(2).

Mikulincer, M., and Shaver, P. (2007). Attachment, group-related processes and psychotherapy. *International Journal of Group Psychotherapy*, *57*(2).

Ormont, L. (2001). *The technique of group treatment. The collected papers of Louis R. Ormont* (Ana Blanco Furgeri, Ed.). Psychosocial.

Raubolt, R.R. (2010). *Theaters of trauma, special edition.* Chapbook Press.

Shedler, J. (2020). Where is the evidence for 'evidence-based' therapy? *Psychiatric Clinics of North America, 41*(2).

Van der Kolk, B.A. (2015). *The body keeps score: Brain, mind and body in the healing of trauma.* Penguin Books.

Yalom, I.D. (1985). *The theory and practice of group psychotherapy* (3rd ed.). Basic Books.

Authors' Biographies

I began my doctoral studies in 1971 with a fellowship at DePaul University in Chicago and completed my PhD in 1978. I began working as a staff psychologist at Pine Rest Mental Health Center in Grand Rapids, Michigan in 1975 and became a licensed clinical psychologist in 1980, at which time I began my private practice. During the last 45 years, I have been an adjunct faculty member at Trinity Christian College, Hope College, Aquinas College, Grand Valley State Colleges, Michigan State University College of Human Medicine, and the Institute for Individual and Group Psychotherapy (IIGP). During this time period, I have had an active practice of individual, group, couples, and family psychotherapy and supervision of other therapists. I have also consulted with mental health agencies, businesses, and regional hospitals. I have been a board member at the Michigan Group Psychotherapy Society and IIGP for the last 20 years. Richard and I supervised our first group of psychotherapists 30 years ago, worked separately for many years, and now have co-led groups for the last 3 years. In April 2021, we began our fourth TGC group.

—Kirk L. Brink, PhD

I am a licensed clinical psychologist and a board-certified psychoanalyst who has been in an independent practice for more than 40 years. I was the founding editor of the online journal *Otherwise*, I served on the board of the International Forum for Psychoanalytic Education for 10 years, and I was elected president of the Michigan Group Psychotherapy Society. In addition, I have provided supervision for the Chinese-American Psychoanalytic Alliance, the Portuguese Association for Psychoanalysis and Psychoanalytic Psychotherapy, Aquinas College, and Michigan State University College of Human Medicine.

I have also published two books, *Power Games* and *Theaters of Trauma Special Edition*, and more than 30 professional papers. With an interest in the interface between social-cultural issues and psychology, I have produced five films, three of which were finalists for the prestigious Gradiva Award. The first, *Detroit: Living in Between*, has recorded 18,000 online views. Filmmaking has led me back to writing and, at times, to mash-up my flash fiction with film. Through this medium and in my publications, I have tried to explore the darker side of human psychology with concision and impact.

—Richard Raubolt, PhD, ABPP

CPSIA information can be obtained
at www.ICGtesting.com
Printed in the USA
LVHW041359170322
713568LV00013B/1469